The

Billionaire

Buddha

THE WISDOM WITHIN
YOUR WALLET

Jane Monica-Jones

Published by Rock Chick 2019

Details for Jane Monica-Jones can be found at
www.janemonicajones.com

ISBN: 978-1-719-27672-6

A PRAYER by Michael Leunig

God bless the lost, the confused,
the unsure, the bewildered, the puzzled,
the mystified, the baffled and the perplexed.

Amen.

ACKNOWLEDGMENTS

Immense appreciation for the many, many people who gave their time to allow me to look at their relationship with money under a metaphoric microscope. And, of course, my ever-courageous clients who have committed to heal their wounds around money. Consequently, they have nobly repaired so many other interconnected aspects of their lives.

Of course, my beloved Costa.

SPECIAL THANKS TO

The *Path of Love*. The most profound personal and
spiritual development process on the planet. It is also the
place where this book had its genesis. Whilst dealing with
a period of severe financial distress and supporting others
in being able to face some of their own distress, the idea
for *The Billionaire Buddha* came to me. I saw clearly how
our relationship with money is forged very early on in our
lives. This understanding and curiosity has set my life on
a course of deep exploration. It's been a gift both to
myself and to my clients. Immense gratitude, for the
Path of Love is always with me.

Also, to my good friend and colleague Paul C Pritchard.
Whose wisdom both in the field of therapy, and the
human condition coupled with the deftness of a poet.
You brought the concepts and ideas of this book to life
with potency and poignancy.

It's has been an honour to work with you and walk along
side of you.

CONTENTS

Invitation to meet your very own
Billionaire Buddha

$

Thank you for investing your curiosity, your money and your time in the great inner adventure of finding your very own **Billionaire Buddha** for financial freedom and financial serenity.

Initially I wanted to call this book **The Wisdom in Your Wallet.** This working title sums up the core theme of my work. In every individual's pocket there is a catalogue of clues and signposts that will reflect back where you are *great* with money, *good enough* with money and where you need to *improve* with money.

What makes this book different from all the other money guides?

Having counselled many people who either want to augment their financial portfolios to people wanting to get out of crippling money scenarios and live debt free, I have seen a clear gap in the market. Many books about financial freedom give you strategies, guidance, loop-hole methods, next-wave fads, property investment advice, share market prophesies and trends, etc. Depending on your personal preference, aptitudes, skills and training, there are many avenues to **make, invest** and **grow money.**

Some of the books out there are outstanding **if** you have the emotional and mental capacity to execute, follow through and adapt within your chosen route. In all the work I have done I haven't met one single person who didn't have room to improve their financial health and psychology.

Time and time again I hear people have bought these books with the very best intentions. But they sit on the bedside table gathering dust and serve as yet another great reminder of their inaction, procrastination, apathy and poor time management. None of these books truly tackle the psychology of money. They are often black and white dogma and written in a stern boot-camp style. The marketing hype propels people to buy them because they make sense, they purport to work for so many, they are on trend, and they are best-sellers.

Mostly they sell to people's emotional belief pattern that they are failing, drowning, miserable, need to change, exhausted, beaten, and now becoming all too commonplace, some are downright desperate or suicidal.

The absence of money, as with physical health, can bring misery, but possessing it is no guarantee of happiness either. What they often miss is the compassionate understanding of the key common denominator in all these stressful equations ... the emotional and mental blocks we all have to some degree around money.

When money and survival enter our adult psyche and reality we act out in ways that often seem incompatible with how we function in other areas of our lives, for example: self-sabotaging, are too afraid to try something new, won't take risks, take ill-informed risks, act without integrity, gamble, over-spend, become miserly, greedy, controlling, manipulating, deceive, become negative, hopeless, and stuck.

For me, there is a better way, a kinder way, a way of objective, balanced and exceptionally real way of looking at your financial personality that ALSO gives you tools of clarity, wisdom and discernment for you to make improvements in all areas of your life. It is only having a clear head, heart and tailored action plan that can bring you into ease, wisdom, discernment and effectiveness with your personal money weave. Only a deep exploration and awareness of your unique psychological blueprint of money can give you the capacity, courage and conviction to make a surmountable change.

We may have many primary relationships: partner, husband, wife, mother, father, children, friends, boss, employees and believe it or not they all involve money. In our society ... money weaves its way through everything. So we'd better get a handle on how to allow money to serve us well. I strongly believe that understanding your own psychology around money is the first step in harnessing its potential for freedom ... then and only then do these other great books make sense and actually have some chance of working for you.

Let's move from *Blindful*, to *Mindful* to *Kindful* in all our money dealings. This is the only way to live a fulfilled life full of promise, potential and prosperity.

In the **Billionaire Buddha** you will discover your true riches through honest self-reflection, exploration of psychological theory and your body~mind balance and your bank balance should all reconcile beautifully.

Ready? Then let's begin.

Introduction

"Money is a singular thing. It ranks with love as Man's greatest source of joy. And with death, as his greatest source of anxiety." ~ John Kenneth Galbraith

£

For most of my life, I have struggled in my relationship with money. If I compare it to a personal relationship, I should have left it many years ago, for all the torture and sense of insanity and misleading illusions it has sometimes thrown at me. This relationship has brought me both heartbreak and ecstasy. A sense of complete security and at times crippling insecurity. Money for me has been an ever-calling siren with whom I have sometimes yielded and sometimes wished she would just shut-up and disappear!

The conditioning of the human psyche begins in the womb. Hundreds of studies confirm the thoughts and emotional states of mothers during pregnancy are transferred to the unborn child via neurohormones. Meaning any and all anxieties, stresses, hopes and fears my mother had about her own financial situation were transferred into my cellular make-up and nervous system. Therefore, I literally imbibed all of my mother's beliefs, thoughts and behaviours about money way before I even got here! There is also evidence that suggests chemical traces from past trauma experienced by both parents before conception are embedded into the semen and ovum DNA; so, our beginnings with money started before we were even just a twinkle in our parents' eyes.

Whether I believe money is a necessary evil, perhaps the source of great happiness or the road to heartache and/or spiritual death — for me it is a relationship that I cannot live without. If I am to participate in this fiscal society then logic dictates that money and I are inextricably linked to the bitter end (I am now changing this to the sweet end).

My story and conditioning with money (post birth) started as the youngest of five girls, growing up in Sydney, Australia, in a middle-class family. At a time when most mothers, as with mine, didn't need to earn an income. Her fulltime relentless job was running the family home and the welfare of my father, the children and herself. My father ran a very successful Law practice in the city.

We had a substantial home with premium Sydney Harbour views, private school education and trips away skiing for our annual holidays. You could say that we were well-off, not rich, but living comfortably, and more comfortably than most. However, there was still a repetitive tone in our household, even with all the trappings of a family doing well, that we were not rich and certainly not rich enough. A tone mainly expressed by my mother, that somehow our family life would be better, even happier, if they had even more money. To accommodate the needs and aspirations of my mother and subsequently their children, my father worked a lot; late nights and many weekends. It felt like my father was mostly absent from my family home life, except for holidays and the occasional weekend. This frustrated my mother with her having to take on the burden of managing five kids 'alone'.

My mother was a kind and compassionate woman. She wasn't acting from a place of entitlement or greed. She was simply caught up in her own conditioning around money and fantasies about how it would make everything better. Yet it did not impede her acts of kindness. Once she took on four children in the neighbourhood whose parents had become very ill. They lived with us for six months. At one point there were ten children living in our house, ranging from twenty to four years old. This put immense stress on my mother and my parents' well-off bank balance. One of the most vivid memories I have of this time, is three shopping trollies filled to overflowing and dinner time being absolutely crazy, children lining up to be fed like a camp mess hall. This exemplifies the simultaneous and often conflicting values and belief systems that we carry within us. It's these dominant beliefs that are running the show and causing havoc. My mother believed there was both never enough and enough to go around.

As we all do, I took on and internalised my

mother's financial stress of wanting more and saw how this thing called money and finances impacted her very existence and emotional and mental health. As for my father, it left a searing impression, which later crystallised into a powerful belief, that to have all that we had, meant my Dad would be absent. In short: I couldn't have it all. There would always be a dark emotional sacrifice to material success.

These are just two examples of how money impacted my childhood and of course there are many more impressions and internalisations, both conscious and unconscious that I adopted and assumed about money. My parents' experiences of money and my subsequent internalisations imprinted a confusing and contradictory relationship with money. Although we had plenty, there was still a sense of not having enough and that a lot more would make my family life more pleasant, stress-free and relaxing. In my innocent and juvenile assumptions, this belief system was framed as:

'If we had more money, my mother would be happier and maybe my father would be around a lot more.'

Subsequently, one of the first ground rules of *my* relationship with money was, *'My family needs a lot of money.'* Which was internalised as *'I need a lot of money.'* This was built as a survival strategy that would save my family and more importantly my sense of safety inside my family structure. *'If my parents are ok, they will be able to take care of me!'*

As an adult, this drove a large portion of my behaviour with money in two very distinct ways. Firstly, a persistent itch/urge and sometimes insane longing to always want heaps more money than I had and secondly the belief that having more would make my suffering go away. That all my problems, exclusive of money, would be solved by having more money. Sound familiar?

Moreover, these drives manifested in some prominent behaviours during my childhood. I continually formulated ideas on how to make money, get money or wrangle money. When I was about eight there was a campaign by the local government looking for any infestation of Argentine Ants. Any discovery of an infestation would result in a financial reward. I became obsessed. Every afternoon after school I scoured the street curbs, looking for ant trails that would lead me to my pot of gold. For three straight weeks I ignored the other kids playing, or perhaps they were down another rabbit hole with their own financial plans to fix their families. To maddening effect, this type of behaviour stuck with me through my early adult years. I would have to catch myself being completely stuck in my head, going around and around, thinking up ways to get money, endlessly wrapping my head around the obsession to make more money! And never understanding the pain or the core emotional wound that these runaway impulses were coming from.

My desire for money (or a sense of safety and peace) also took on more disturbing patterns. I frequently stole money from my parents' wallets. The impulses sometimes became bigger than me or any sense of right or wrong or consequences. Simply having some money, more money, a stash of money made me feel calmer. Of course, I was not aware of this behaviour in any psychological or emotional sense. So prolific was my stealing, particularly in my youth, that around the age of fourteen, after discovering that I had again stolen money from her wallet, my mother bundled me into the car, parked outside a juvenile detention centre a couple of suburbs away, and told me very sternly that this would be my future.

This memory now brings up great sadness and distress for the younger me. I felt so helpless as I couldn't control what I was doing — I knew it was wrong and I just couldn't help myself. I can remember that kid so fearful that she might one day end up in prison for a behaviour she felt she was unable to control. In all those many years, every time I put my hand in somewhere it shouldn't have been, I would have two voices screaming in my head — *'Don't do this, this is not right, this is not good!'* and the other *'Yes go on, I need it.'* The compulsive behaviour is clear now. I've done a lot of self-reflection and self-inquiry to get to a deeper understanding. I have sort to heal and unpack my own complex relationship with money and it has shone a light on so much more of the dysfunction of my initial conditioning around value and worth and more importantly self-value and self-worth.

In retrospect, it feels like I was somehow psychologically possessed, unable to break free. Like most addiction or compulsive behaviour, I was drowning. This dramatically affected my self-esteem, my impulse control and my overall happiness and wellbeing.

I still feel the sense of shame and pain of having this behaviour in my past and it has taken a long time to fully understand it all. It is not surprising that I have become a Financial Therapist … we often teach what we know. And pain and suffering around money is something

I truly know!

Thinking about this time, both as a child and in my early adult life, there was this *same* feeling. The same feeling when I stole money and when I would try to come up with ways to make money — this feeling at its core was an intense feeling of lack. A greater lack that sits more profoundly than just the lack of money. The kind of lack that no amount of money will ever truly fulfil. A hole in my very nature that I believed would be filled by money, success, love, food, power or whatever else I would reach for when I felt overwhelmed with this sense of incomplete or broken me. It was like a great existential hole opening within me and swallowing me up. Except without the language I'm giving it now. Without the language it just showed up as the very edges of anxiety, fear and terror. So as not to feel them I would avoid this sensation by acting out. Without any support or awareness, this hole deluded me into believing that money (in my specific case) will fill in this hole, this defect, this fundamental flaw and I won't have to fall into the pain or annihilation of it. It sounds dramatic, perhaps too dramatic ... but this is why people are self-harming in all sorts of disproportionate ways. And yes, for a while it offers some relief. It's that fix we've habitually yearned for. But it never lasts long.

For me, the lack of security that my mother was going to be okay, and hence I would be okay and taken care of as a child, and a longing for my father to be more present at home drove me to near insanity. The stealing behaviour and incessant formulations and strategies to make a quick dollar were my survival strategies to try to plug that hole in an insecure environment. But of course, I could not reconcile that as a child or young adult. Understanding our unique psychological relationship with money means going back and looking for the faulty or second-rate wiring and giving it a more appropriate 'adult' upgrade. For me it is clear that my reckless and fear-driven child was running my money show … night after night the curtain came down to no applause and as I got older, it turned to hissing and booing with no reprieve.

Your story might not seem as dramatic or obvious as mine, most wiring around money is more subtle, more covert — I work on those belief systems too. I have had to investigate, inquire, and ultimately overcome my demons around money. To be ruthlessly honest and face myself. It's a life-long journey of being vigilant and reminding myself that I have more self-worth and self-value than any amount of net-value or net-worth. Money continues to teach me so much … money is always reflecting my *Billionaire Buddha* Psyche.

"Inviting our thoughts and feelings into awareness allows us to learn from them rather than be driven by them." ~ Dan Siegel

As a Financial Therapist I see directly so much torture and pain around people's relationship with money. And happily, after some guidance and sometimes some hard-hitting truths, I have seen people change their lives in so, so many repercussive ways. I've helped people re-gain ground, build a rocket ship and fly … even those who have lost everything in messy divorce settlements. When your own relationship with money moves from **Blindful** to **Mindful**, so do the dynamics within your romantic relationship (it helps significantly when both parties do the work). If you're single and looking for a partner, it can help you find the right match. Trust me … clearing out this issue will reverberate deep into every aspect of your life.

So often we only look at the utilitarian quality of money and its usefulness in satisfying our needs and wants. When we choose to delve a little deeper and understand our direct relationship with money, the narrative focusses primarily on how we can accumulate more of it and little focus is put on our core beliefs, values and behaviours around money. Examining, in a safe and constructive manner, all the ways we engage our old and redundant belief systems that run our lives is both challenging and liberating. We can truly set ourselves free by examining our wallets and how we live out our money-dramas.

Unfortunately, we do not look at how our childhood conditioning experience has driven our behaviours with money. Emotional landscapes within psychotherapy are usually chartered to clear emotional blocks: for the good of saving marriages; saving ourselves from addiction; harmonising a relationship; to find love; to be a better parent etc. Rarely, if at all, do people seek therapeutic intervention solely to get a better understanding of their financial landscapes. Why is that? It leaves me baffled when I see our current societal beliefs and practices around money fall incomprehensibly short of sustainable and balanced well-being for our species and our planet. In ignoring this financial toxic pandemic, we continue to exacerbate our chronic cultural unhappiness. Money cannot buy happiness, but happiness can create relative and healthy wealth.

I am betting most of us believe that if we had more money, a lot of our problems would be solved? For a long time, I was an avid believer of this too. The pain of my own money behaviour escalated to such an extent that I could no longer live with my own contradictory and polarised emotions. I was constantly broke or had large amounts of money that I let slip through my fingers. I went from one extreme to the other. I had no real security and most importantly I had no real peace of mind. I made a strong commitment to myself to tackle this once and for all. I could never have predicted how difficult it was to start and how easy it was to solve.

When we are not run by our negative conditioning around money, the accumulation of it or lack of it, we can then put money into its rightful place — as a great teacher and a currency for change.

Money is important. It is not important because it gives us importance, but rather it is a teacher for the soul — that instructs us to be **Mindful** and **Kindful**.

ii

This book is divided into two parts. The Theory and The Workbook. It depends on your learning style as to which way you will approach the book. I suggest that you read a chapter of the theory and then spend some dedicated time with the workbook. Within the theory part of the book there will be self-enquiry contemplations. These are designed to help you unlock the mechanics that you operate with, in your past and present relationship with money. The workbook is a *28 Day Challenge* to explore, discover and express your financial personality. If you have the luxury (and in many cases the necessity) of seeing a good holistic counsellor or relational therapist, you may want to share your findings with them. Of course, you are very welcome to come and work with me. Them and I can help you navigate the fog and the clarity with an objective perspective. It's called a *28 Day Challenge* for a reason. And it is my sincere wish that at the end of the 28 days you will have a greater understanding of your relationship with money. If you truly dedicate some time to the enquiry you will experience dramatic changes in how you relate to all aspects of your life where money is woven. Work hard, be courageous and don't short-change yourself. When we raise our self-worth, we have every possibility of raising our net-worth.

Chapter 1

THE PSYCHOLOGY OF MONEY

"We must use money in order to study ourselves as we are and as we can become." ~ Jacob Needleman

₽

    In primitive times our source of survival came from the contribution we gave to our tribe in the hunting and gathering of food and making of clothing and shelter etc. Historically our input was most likely devoid of the intensity of the psychological associations of survival we experience today. Alongside our survival instinct, i.e., keeping the body alive and healthy, we have linked various complex and interwoven psychological associations with money and survival. Associations that distort our natural and primal survival motivations, for example, envy, shame, desire for a sense of power, pleasure, pride and everything in between. Everything that motivates us to go to work, earn money and even to rob a bank, (beyond filling our bellies) are powerful psychological imprints that were laid down in our early childhood experiences.

"So the instinct for survival, which translates into fear of annihilation and death, is the energy behind adaptation and hence, conditioning. The child finds himself in the situation of having to be what his environment (parents) dictates in order for him to survive. So we can say that it is due to the instinct for self-preservation that acquiescence to the coercive forces in the environment occurs." ~ A.H. Almaas

Almaas illustrates that we have become conditioned by our environment as a strategy to survive. Through the need to adapt to our initial environment, our essential qualities and needs, the intrinsic self that may have differed from our parents, were shaped, moulded and twisted into something that matched more of the parents' desires rather than what is the expression of our true self.

We became conditioned to think, behave and believe in accordance with external forces — *'If I make mum/dad happy; if I am good, better, the best, then I will be taken care of. So I must subjugate my essential needs and desires and set to the task of what I think mum/dad may want.'*

"The child adopts his parents' values and attitudes or rebels. In either case, he is conditioned to be and to act in certain ways, which, through the passage of time, become so ingrained that he takes them to be his identity. Slowly he forgets his true identity and becomes what he is being conditioned to be and to believe." ~ A.H. Almaas

As we grow the forces and authorities from our childhood — parents, school, teachers, peers, and society, all dictate what our norm of survival should look like. Even fashion trends, pop music and popular culture all inform our norm. And all the while our bank balance is also bowing under pressure to keep up with external forces and influence. Through all of this, we lost our essential self: the self that wanted to be a lion tamer and ended up being an accountant to survive. The self that became a brain surgeon when all we wanted to do was live in Tuscany and write novels.

Money is inextricably linked to our survival. In simplistic terms, money is the device by which we can acquire our basic needs to survive — providing all that is necessary, i.e., food, shelter and clothing for the preservation of the body for as long as possible. If we look at money in psychological terms, it goes beyond just a device for survival. Money becomes both a conceptual maze and a tangible web that is loaded with our projections, our beliefs, hopes and fears. Having the perceived healthy amount of money or not attaining it has a dramatic stamp on our psychological well-being; and therefore, naturally our health.

"Money is like the id itself, the primordially repressed, the collective unconscious appearing in specific denominations." ~ James Hillman

Money moves from its purely utilitarian quality for survival to something that can be the cause of either psychological pleasure or pain: which varies wildly in its significance from person to person. Beyond its use as a survival mechanism, money is often viewed as a tool for

3

the enhancement of status, power, self-worth and a sense of importance, and even purpose.

In my Financial Therapy practice I often see what may appear to be a simple financial issue, for example, not being able to save, is really masking a self-worth or self-care issue. One particular client I had been working with for a couple of months, was exceptionally distressed at her inability to save. Although she was on an excellent pay package, by the time her next pay cheque came through, she had spent all her money. She was spending on ephemeral items or indulgent experiences, fashion items, expensive dinners, wines, socialising etc. When all along longing to buy a home in the future yet liberally spending the deposit.

With an enquiry into her history, we discovered that her parents lived quite humbly, with not much spare cash floating around. On the odd occasion, when there was a little extra cash, she had often seen her mother promptly snatch the dollars from her father's hand and go out and purchase something frivolous for herself.

This made my client feel that she and everyone else in the household were missing out on a little something extra for themselves. Subsequently, she adopted her mother's clothes spending habit. When discussing the feelings she experienced when buying more clothes that she didn't need, a familiar voice would always pop into her head, *'But I am worth it.'* It appeared the client in those foundational experiences with her mother and money, felt unseen and unworthy, as though she wasn't allowed anything extra in her humble upbringing. As an adult she took that little extra left over after her expenses and treated herself just as her mother had done, buying a little bit of self-worth, if you will. As we unlinked her self-esteem from her material purchases her drive to spend on clothing and other indulgent experiences decreased and she started saving for the first time in her life.

Most of our conditioning and the ways we behave with money are generally unconscious, unless they cause direct mental anguish and pain. Some conditioning may be a little sneakier to recognise, giving the appearance of functioning normally with money. There are many manifestations of a flawed psychological conditioning from our foundational years with regards to money: overspending, retail therapy, not being able to save, gambling, underearning, overworking and even over accumulation. The list goes on. Some dramatic and overt and some subtle and insidious.

A dynamic I often see is couples having financial challenges with opposing views and values around money and financial priorities.

One couple had the typical scenario whereby the one party, in this case the husband, was putting an incredible amount of time into his job, working late nights and weekends. Of course, this caused a rift in the relationship as the wife felt her husband was never at home. He wanted to provide really well for his family and felt he was expected to do so. Looking a little closer at their situation, the long hours away from his family meant there was little time for connection with his wife and kids. As such, this wife was 'treating herself' by shopping for expensive things for the house as a compensation for having little meaningful contact with her husband. The default argument for him was, *'If you didn't keep buying so much stuff, I wouldn't have to work so long to pay for it all!'* Catch 22.

During our time together, it was revealed that the husband had had a very dysfunctional home life as a child, with a violent alcoholic father who was often out of work and at home a lot of the time. Consequently, the husband viewed family life as potentially dangerous. He feared on some level that spending too much time at home might bring out some previously unexpressed violent tendencies inherited from his father. Working long hours became an unconscious refuge for him and also created a perceived safety for his wife and kids. Perversely, spending plenty of time at work became his safety zone for protecting his family; potentially from himself.

As you can guess, couples are a large part of my Financial Therapy practice. Not only do we have money issues of our own but throw a partner into the mix with their unique history and we add multiple layers of complexity to our issues or problems with money.

We of course bring to our relationships our healthy money-selves and our unhealthy money-selves. The unhealthy parts are predominately hidden. In therapeutic terms these parts are called blindspots. They are often glaringly obvious to our friends, family and colleagues. And we move through life oblivious to them. Until that 'ahah' moment arrives (welcome or unwelcome) and the veil is lifted. Financial Blindspots are often more painful to discover as they are intertwined with so much of how we view ourselves; our image management and identity. Inquiring into our self-perception and ideas of the self can be quite scary. As with all forms of self-discovery and self-inquiry it's better to have a soft place to fall and an experienced gentle hand to guide you.

In the initial research stages of this book it was challenging to find people to interview about their views on money and how they see themselves when dealing with money. There seemed to be a Financial Blindspot beyond their initial predictive statement of, *'I would certainly like a little more.'*

Even Freud had a little something to say on the subject:

"... money questions will be treated by cultured people in the same manner as sexual matters, with the same inconsistency, prudishness and hypocrisy."
~ Sigmund Freud

Just as challenging a subject like sex and sexuality, discussing money and finances can often be deflected, carry shame and cover deeper meanings than just wanting 'a little more.' You might feel better to know that even the godfather of psychoanalysis was not immune to Financial Blindspots.

On Freud **" ... he remained as blind about his own relationship to money as many of us are today about ours. Referring to his father's financial setbacks, he admitted that he preferred to suppress rather than explore their impact on him. "** ~ Richard Trachtman

₽

Chapter 2

MONEY & PAIN

"I like to be in pain when I'm getting massaged.
That way I know I'm getting my money's worth."
~ Alison Brie

∩

The first noble truth of Buddhism is 'Life is Suffering.'

Not a cheery thought I know, but let's look at what this truly means and how this can be reflected in our relationship with money. Suffering in the discourse of Buddhist teachings does not mean *all* life is suffering. Of course, there is much beauty, happiness and joy that we can experience in many moments of our life.

Suffering is the existential crisis we experience when we fully consider that there is impermanence and imperfection in all things. Life is not infinite and lasting. A cut flower will eventually die, a relationship may end by either party or by death and wealth may not be permanent — every stock market crash is a testament to this. This premise sits in our psyche as dissatisfaction and unease — or we could say, we suffer because of the uncomfortable nature of this contemplation.

It is not unusual that we use money as a tool to try and battle against this untenable premise. A somewhat misplaced example closely associated with our existential crisis is the beauty industry that is built on our desire to fight the inevitable ageing process. Trying as we might to beat it back with a stick of cream, when not so skin deep we all know that decay will be our end.

In clinical terms, we call the avoidance of pain and suffering Experiential Avoidance or EA. We employ EA when we try to avoid painful memories, thoughts, feelings, physical sensations and other internal experiences. When EA becomes habit, or the norm, the results are body dysmorphic disorders: eating disorders, pathological gambling, porn addiction, substance abuse, excessive over-exercise, depression, anxiety and PTSD, for example. Over-working can also be a strategy to avoid pain. Obsessional spending on expensive items so as to appear within a higher financial class could also be on that list. There are many and varied ways of compensating or acting out so as not to feel the pain. Even our obsession with our mobile devices and social media is a way we avoid our internal experience. You only have to look at faces falling into devices in any given public space to see there is a zombie-like disconnect. What we are really seeing here is our inability to just *Be*. We are compelled, always to *Do* something.

Experiencing our feelings, particularly those that are not positive, can be very uncomfortable for us and sometimes even excruciating with the deeper emotions. Obviously feeling happy brings about relaxation in the body and our thought processes quieten, feeling less burdensome and worrying. But beyond the pleasant effects of the feelings of happiness and contentment, we have a cluster of reasons why we may be unable to cope with feelings beyond a happy disposition.

These reasons have their source in our infancy. As newborns and tiny babies, our nervous systems were still extremely underdeveloped. All our coping and defence mechanisms such as rationalisation, avoidance and self-regulation that protect our nervous system as older children and as adults have not yet come into play. So when we felt something painful, it was experienced as sheer pain rushing through our bodies, totally consuming us. Take a look at a little one in the throes of crying, it is indeed a full body experience, that they are unable to regulate. This will only be subdued when the source of pain is gone, or they are soothed by an external regulator (mother or father).

The impact of trauma, be it horrendous or apparently harmless, is experienced more profoundly in our infancy than in older children or even in adulthood.

We were so sensitive to our environment as infants that all difficulties in our households or other events were keenly imprinted on our tiny little baby self.

"Trauma can result not only from catastrophic events such as abuse and violence, but incidents that generate effects that are often minimised, such as

minor auto accidents, invasive medical and surgical procedures, divorce, separations and falls - even from something as seemingly benign as a bicycle!"
~ Peter Levine & Maggie Kline

Our general inability to be with pain is reflected most poignantly in our lack of support when experiencing pain or suffering: this deeply shapes our own relationship with pain, and therefore survival and therefore life (and money).

One of the burning complexities of being human is that no-one can really meet us (in live empathy) when we are directly experiencing pain, specifically emotional pain. They may be able to sit beside us, give us a hug, wipe our tears. But step directly into the pain with us? Unfortunately no. Individual pain is a lonely experience.

It has been like this from the beginning. Not only as infants but also as the developing child and it stays with us as adults too. We have never really been taught how to be with our emotional pain when it arises. Most of the strategies given by our well-meaning carers were for pain to be placated as soon as possible. So we learnt strategies of avoidance, running over our feelings or getting busy, which only really prolongs and does not heal the pain. And of course with the advancement of science and medicine we can simply take a pill and make the pain go away. The abuse of medication to suppress the expression of our emotional and physical pain is at pandemic proportions. We do ourselves a great disservice in not being able to be with pain and learn from it. Of course some medical and even emotional conditions demand the use of opiates and anaesthetics, but as a society we must look at what we are teaching our species and our DNA about our relationship to pain. I encounter this acute emotional pain avoidance every day in the therapeutic process.

Clients come to see me because they are experiencing an issue in their life that is causing them emotional distress in some way. As therapists, we support the client to really open to and welcome the painful aspects of their lives as a way to move forward. In the therapeutic process, we essentially encourage a whole spectrum of emotions — anger, sadness and frustration as a way of acknowledging what is genuinely felt by the client and to provide space for these feelings, which they may not often allow for themselves in their day to day lives.

Almost every time with a new client or one who is very new to the therapy process, particularly when they have been recounting an experience that is painful, frustrating, fills them with anger etc. they will suddenly stop and say something like, *'Sorry, I know I am sounding bad, negative, wrong ...'* I recognise it is a defence mechanism of showing their true feelings. Proceeding that moment, when the client has revealed themselves in some way, there is cognitive self-reflective awareness, where the client feels they are somehow 'not allowed' to feel what they are feeling. The feeling most often experienced is a sense of shame. Shame in their felt truth — in what is true for them in that moment in the therapy session.

So why is this? For many and various reasons, as children most of us were unable or more correctly 'not allowed' to express large negative emotions. As tiny babies, we often cried out passionately and with full force, when we felt uncomfortable or in pain in some way. As we grew, we started to modify this powerful natural behaviour when we became cognisant of the disapproving responses from the outside world.

Maybe Mum would get frustrated or overwhelmed when we were being our passionate crying self. So we learned to modify this behaviour and to subdue our authentic selves and feelings in order to continue having our needs met. When we cried out, and there was no-one there, either emotionally or physically, we soon learned that crying was of no use.

As we grew, our tantrums, hissy fits and melts downs, may have been ignored, ridiculed or punished. When we were upset or sad, maybe Mum didn't have time to really support us or sense our pain because she had other kids, other tasks or was overwhelmed in some way. Consequently, anything to do with expressing pain or our larger emotions, we quickly learned, was a no-go zone or no-one will genuinely be there for us, and we naturally brought this strategy into adulthood.

Although our parents may have been justified, in getting us to stop our larger emotions, either for our protection or as a form of behavioural modification, what is felt by us as children is, we are not allowed to feel our authentic feelings. In other cases where the child may have been in a very angry and violent environment, tapping into pain is a direct route to what was witnessed as a child, which of course reminds the child that no-one was there to protect them from all of this.

Every time we were told to get over it, stop that behaviour, not had a sympathetic present ear, not held, or not had space for our pain and feelings, what was laid down in our nervous system was *the feelings I feel as a kid are somehow wrong.'* So when large and painful emotions arise in us as adults, it is as though we hear that parent in our head, and then stop ourselves: *'I am sounding bad, negative or wrong … I will not be loveable, and my needs won't be met, and I therefore will not survive.'*

"Mental and emotional health follows the nervous system." ~ Peter Levine

If the nervous system is wired with suppressed emotions it is fair to say that within our nervous system blueprint there will be many glitches. When we don't deal with our emotions in a clean and self-owning way, meaning; *'I am angry at what is happening'* rather than *'You are making me angry'*, one of two things happen: we become a ticking time bomb, or we become the placated walking dead.

How different cultures grieve, and express grief is testament to how we 'learn' a set of codes and cultural norms to be acceptable within our given environment. Some Middle Eastern cultures will wail and sob with such force that it can look bewildering, even frightening, in comparison to an Australian way of expressing grief. Similarly the British and American standard for grief is often private and not public.

Our pain both historical and present needs to go somewhere; needs to be exposed to the sunlight in some way. Or we will either completely explode, as we see in violent behaviour or implode becoming the walking dead. The massive numbers of those experiencing depression and anxiety illustrate this. Avoiding our emotions and pain doesn't mean they dissipate; this pent-up energy has to go somewhere. It will usually come out sideways in constant complaining, frustration and blaming others. Or aggressive or passive aggressive behaviours.

A business owner came to see me complaining that the entire time he had been in business, although successful, was filled with endless aggravation, frustration and the occasional lawsuit, that kept him stressed and at his wit's end. He expressed he had a friend in the same field and the same level of success, who seemed to have no such problems. To his credit, he started to wonder that maybe there was something in his relationship with money and earning that vastly differed from his friend.

After working together for a few sessions, we happened upon an intriguing discovery. I asked my client whether he liked the work he was doing. He took a long pause, then a sigh and turned to me and said, *'I fucking hate it!'*

Shaking his head slightly he continued *'When my father died, I was just finishing school. Although I saw myself going to university, with his early death, there was no way that was going to happen.'* My client started to touch upon this painful period in his life.

'I fought my Mum a lot in this period, trying to convince her that I could pay my way, but she wouldn't have it and finally she convinced me to do the work my father did. I didn't want to keep fighting her, she had enough on her plate.' In our next session, my client's first words, even before he sat down were, *'You know, I have a lot of anger towards my parents, that I didn't even*

realise.' He went on, *'I get that I can't blame my Dad, but somehow I am angry at him for dying when he did, things might have turned out differently for me.'* He continued *'As for my Mum, she wouldn't trust me...I think I am getting why there are so many problems in my working life.'*

My client's foundational period of establishing his way in the world was fraught with the trauma of losing his father and appeasing his mother. Years later he found himself in a career that he absolutely hated. Finally, he saw how much suppressed anger and despair filled his working life. He had projected all the unexpressed pain on to the way he dealt with his business. This meant he often had personality clashes, was controlling and continuously micromanaging. He was sometimes unreasonable with debtors and was quick to take people to court.

After dealing with his old grief for his father that he had never acknowledged or expressed and using a compassion practice whereby he could experience what was going on for his mother, he started to feel some self-compassion for where he had landed in his career.

Not long afterward he expressed that things had started to become a bit more pleasant for him at work. *'I think I am starting not to hate my work so much,'* he said. *'I am letting things go more and allowing things to work out the way they will without me having to control it so much.'*

"After trauma the world is experienced with a different nervous system. The survivor's energy now becomes focused on suppressing inner chaos, at the expense of spontaneous involvement..."
~ Bessel van der Kolk

Giving space to the pain my client had held in for so many years meant that his worldview started to change. His external circumstances had not changed, he still earned a living the same way, yet through healing some of his old pain his work life became less painful.

We often look only at the external results of our relationship with money — it being a challenge, elusive, erratic or even having us living on struggle street. Our ability to earn, survive or even thrive is very rarely considered in the context of our personal histories. Money is more than a numbers game — it is the sum total of our histories which we project onto our realities.

"Economists have calculated that every dollar invested in high-quality home visitation, day care, and preschool programs results in seven dollars of savings on welfare payments, health-care costs, substance-abuse treatment, and incarceration, plus higher tax revenues due to better-paying jobs."
~ Bessel van der Kolk

Now that's worth thinking about!

Chapter 3

MONEY & SHAME

"Until you make the unconscious conscious, it will direct your life and you will call it fate." ~ Carl Jung

₮

For research purposes, I created a quick website to capture 'little money secrets.' I encouraged people to share secrets anonymously about themselves and money. Secrets they are unwilling to share openly with people around them.

Below are some of the examples of people's little money secrets …

'I really hate myself that I am so bad with money.'

'Many years ago, as part of my job, I used to have to take the money from the till at work to the bank. I organised for

my friend to give me a bit of a beating on route and took the cash. We split the $5500.'

'I steal money out of the till at work. They pay me shit, so I deserve it.'

'I really believed I was going to be rich in this life. I don't know what went wrong, I just can't seem to catch a break.'

'I continually spend more money than I make. It's so stressful!'

From the many and varied responses, I discovered two amazing things. Firstly, so many people hold secrets about money ... in fact, heaps of them. I had over 50 answers within 15 minutes of putting the call out on social media. And secondly, there is so much pain and emotional complexities locked up behind those responses.

One particular feeling or emotion that is often experienced by many of us particularly in relation to money, is a sense of shame.

Shame is probably the most intense emotion we can experience and is an emotional state we most want to avoid. It is a feeling that somehow, we are fundamentally flawed. Amazingly these courageous souls shared their money secrets and it convinces me how many of us (if not all) have some shame around our relationship with money or certain aspects of it. And more importantly we would like to take ownership of it and be free of it.

Shame touches within us a fear of being rejected. If a specific shameful element of our self is revealed or seen we may not be included, loved, respected or even wanted. Although extremely uncomfortable and even painful, there is an evolutionary reason for shame. Shame is a psychological mechanism that was developed to trigger the individual to conform to the ways of the tribe.

"The function of pain is to prevent us from damaging our own tissue. The function of shame is to prevent us from damaging our social relationships, or to motivate us to repair them."
~ Daniel Sznycer

To try and rally against any event that will lead to shame we created what is known by various names within therapeutic fields, as … the Super Ego, the Inner Critic, the Critical Inner Voice or the Judge … just to name a few.

The function of this voice in our head is to point out when we are wrong, bad, inadequate or guilty in various ways so that we can modify our behaviour. Although this may sound like a sharp mean voice, you have to remember its purpose was to get us to follow the rules of our first home environment as a strategy to survive within our tribe. This voice had its mission of making us follow the rules when we were growing up so that we learned that stealing, for example, isn't acceptable by the tribe. Continuing this example when we stole and got caught, we were punished and/or disciplined as a child. Then as we grew and maintained the behaviour of stealing, we later adopted our own self-disciplinary role, having the judge in our head condemn us for our conduct. When this inner voice is gently speaking the truth and guiding us, it becomes an ally. When its messages are painful and aggressive, chances are it is not aligned to serve us in the current situation … this if often called negative self-talk. Unfortunately, some of the rules that were laid down about money in our childhoods may not function so well for us as adults.

Most of the rules we had to follow as children were reasonable … stealing is generally considered a no-go zone in all tribes. In a way, shame is meant to motivate us to reconnect with our tribe and its rules. We often give shame a lousy rap. Firstly, because it is a felt emotion that we wouldn't want to wish upon ourselves and secondly, because of how the inner critic can sometimes be debilitating. Although, if we look at shame objectively, it is a device that gets us conforming to social and cultural norms. In survival terms it keeps us safe.

Let us take the example of the common expressions or views about people who are rich. In a way the following opinion is a 'rule' of sorts. A large group of people might believe that all rich people are greedy, selfish, mean and self-serving. Imagine for a moment that this statement was often expressed in your childhood growing up. Fast forward a few years and you start earning a good income, even a very good one, but it just isn't making you happy for some reason.

Maybe something inside is nagging at you, an inner voice, sometimes whispering that it's just not right or perhaps shameful for you to be making all this money. You may have reoccurring feelings of guilt for making more money than others. Or you may feel so terrible about being richer than other people that you unconsciously sabotage yourself and lose vast sums of money ensuring that you don't become one of those 'terrible rich people.' Are you getting the picture? This is a simplistic example, but you can hopefully see that the foundational conditioning for our hero was, rich people are bad people. So if our hero becomes rich, he will start to believe that somehow, he is a bad person too. That having money and being a good person are incompatible. Most of the foundational conditioning we possess is generally unconscious. That is to say, it quietly runs the show in the shadows. It is usually only in the therapeutic setting that we start to uncover a little of what is hidden from us. By slowly illuminating the shadows we can come into the light of healing.

When I began my Financial Therapy practice it took a little while for people to get their head around what I was doing. *'Oh, so you are like a financial planner'*, would be their first response. Or *'You help people to become wealthy, right!?'* Although clients may and do become wealthy after working with me, this is really a by-product of what I do. Mostly, I get people to analyse, assess and heal the areas in their relationship with money that cause them to suffer. This has ramifications on a deeper level and positively influences their whole dynamic with survival, self-care and self-responsibility. In short … I can change their entire lives for the better.

One thing I definitely know from doing this work is that it's hard to get people to talk about themselves and money. Superficially they can talk, even brag. But the very frank, real and unadulterated conversation about themselves and money is so alien to our culture that it takes time to learn the honest language of money. I believe on some level, there is a 'collective secret' that says, we should all have a good handle on money as we grow into adulthood. Yet we are generally never taught about managing money, let alone how our individual psychology may affect our relationship with it. As such, money and the discussion of it, is in a way, the last taboo and … as with any taboo it is going to be rife with shame.

My belief is that this conversation, particularly in these times, just might be the gateway we need for personal and planetary survival.

I always ask people *'How are you and money?'* One of the first go-to responses I receive from people is, *'We/I don't talk about money'*. In other circumstances, this of course usually shuts the whole conversation down — except with me. I am somewhat of a brave soul and I don't let them off so lightly and will often have them talking about why they don't talk about money in no time at all! The *'I don't talk about money'* response is an absolutely fascinating one which makes me think it harks back to simpler times when it was vulgar or crass to talk about money. There was a time when it was vulgar and crass to talk about sex and sexuality. We've come a long way in recognising that open, clear and honest conversations about sex only breeds acceptance, tolerance and a deeper understanding of the diversity of human beings.

It is the kind of response that implies *'not a conversation for polite society.'* But if we look deeper at *'We don't talk about money'* or *'I don't talk about money'* what is being demonstrated is an intentional choice to be identified as polite society, not vulgar and crass. In other words it shows a conformist to a possibly very outdated code of societal conduct. When in truth … the conversation can set many free. Debt, mismanagement of money, the loss of it etc. are deemed as chronic failings. Again, the same prevents the conversation for learning and recovery. Let's keep talking about money in safe and supportive environments so we can find new and productive ways to use money for good and for positive change.

Our refusal to have the difficult conversation around money means we have created an identity that is unwilling or fixed. Any fixed identity will only succeed in a fixed universe. As the only constant is change … it's always prudent to be flexible with identity and fixed ideas.

In the Great Depression, for example, there were people on both sides of the scale — those who struggled and those who saw others struggle. Perhaps your great, great grandfather struggled. It would have been pretty hard to talk about money in those times, right? So it got entrenched as a particular behaviour, *'We don't talk about money.'* These subliminal messages are often passed blindly down through the generations until they land with you. You feel no affiliation whatsoever with his direct experience but somehow, you've embodied his beliefs. Most of these converging beliefs and codes are contradictory. Many people hold two polarised beliefs at the same time: *'all good things come to those who wait'* and *'the early bird catches the worm.'* We are flooded with opposing viewpoints that leave us in the realms of procrastination, frustration and inertia. Unless we unravel the mess, we will remain in the mess.

The same could also be said about religious traditions and money. I often see a similar form of what I would call behavioural rigidity when people combine their religious beliefs and money. One such client was turning herself inside out trying to rectify her religious beliefs and the acquisition of money. She believed that saintliness, even Godliness, was linked to poverty. Many times in our sessions, when contemplating the possibility of having more money, she would quickly cut herself short, feeling ashamed that there was something wrong with her for wanting more; more than God's plan for a life lived in poverty. She was a smart businesswoman who wanted a more affluent lifestyle. But every time her natural talents gave her the abundance and freedom, she desired she felt like a sinner. She felt like the camel trying to pass through the eye of a needle to get into the kingdom of God.

After some time she discovered that maybe this was just a 'belief system'. Although apparently a noble one, it kept her constantly on struggle street, stressed and as she would say, *'pissed off'*. One day she expressed to me *'I am not the nicest person when I am struggling financially. I am angry and a horror to be around. I hardly feel I can do God's work when I am in this situation.'* And in that moment the camel slipped through the eye of the needle. She understood that she could do more good with money than without it as she was a naturally altruistic and charitable person.

Confusion and shame about who we believe ourselves to be and money were alive in the early days of psychoanalysis. Freud connected money with faeces in the study of his patient he called the Ratman. Conjuring ideas that money is somewhat dirty. From here it is just a short step to such terms as the 'filthy rich' or 'filthy lucre'. It is no wonder we have strained and complex relationships with money.

Shame and money are reflected when our businesses fail. When we go bankrupt or when we look soberly at our bad debt. When we experience a very public financial loss or when we can't provide for our family. It can be present when we have to ask to borrow some money or when we worry about our retirement. Shame is there when we steal money, cheat money and embezzle money. So painful is our shame with money that it makes people jump out of windows when the stock market goes bust. What does suicide and money tell us? What is the fixed belief or identity? *'I am nothing without money'* ... *'I cannot live without money'* ... *'I cannot live with the shame of my perceived failing'.*

In an affluent country such as Australia, with a population of 25 million, at any moment millions of Aussies are experiencing a sense of shame with their financial situation. The following facts could easily be reflected in any affluent nation. The figures may vary slightly but the themes are constant.

There are 2,265,000 Aussies who live in households below the poverty line. Included in that number are 575,000 children who will grow up with the psychological effects of living in this way. At any given night there are 110,000 people who will experience the traumatising effects of sleeping rough in cities all across Australia. There will be 30,161 Aussies who will be facing bankruptcy or insolvency and 198,133 that will become retrenched this year. Now, let's pick the lower figure of 80,000 from the 80,000 to 160,000 of Australian adults experiencing significant problems with gambling and all the associated shame from this addiction.

What about the 956,000 Downunderers experiencing mortgage stress, having to say 'no' to their kids for that new toy or bike. Behind that 'no' expressed to their child is a sense of shame.

In 2016 there were 188,756 recorded instances of unlawful entry in Australia. Let's put this figure down as 188,756 individuals. This does not include those putting their hands in the tills at work, white collar crime or any forms of embezzlement. Whether they are able to admit or acknowledge their shame, the pure act of stealing in any form is a catalyst for experiencing financial shame or its corrupt opposite — a false sense of entitlement.

In total from these figures alone we have above 3.83 million Australians experiencing some form of financial shame. If we take the adult population at around 20 million people, that is almost 20% of the population. Significant huh?! I am illustrating these numbers so that you can get a sense that we are all significantly impacted in an adverse way with the fallout from shame around money.

The only real shame is that we as a society are failing to grasp the urgency of the money/shame spiral in an effective time frame. Capitalism looks great on a spread sheet. But when we throw in humans and emotions the equations look shaky. And the results simply don't add up. Personal and societal money reform is paramount. Let's start where we can … with ourselves and the discovery and exposure of our own misaligned belief systems around money.

Ready to dig deeper into the wisdom in your wallet?

Chapter 4

MONEY & POWER

"A wise person should have money in their head, but not in their heart." ~ Jonathan Swift

K

Money and power are one of the most interesting associations or linkages there is. It is often not considered objectively enough i.e. what are our issues in relation to a sense of power and how do we project this on to money?

Generally, we only contemplate the by-product of this relationship; how we may feel empowered or disempowered around money. We give little thought to how or why we may feel this way. One of the best places to begin looking at the complexity of money and power is through what is known as Infantile Omnipotence.

Infantile Omnipotence developed by psychiatrist Margaret Mahler, is the greatly exaggerated sense of self-importance particular to the development in small children. The feeling of being the centre of the universe experienced by very young children as they separate and individuate from mother. The standpoint, if you will, from the infant is a highly ego-centric stance for survival. *'As I move away from mother, and come into identifying myself as separate from her, my instinctual drive is for self-preservation and as such I place myself at the centre of the universe, blissfully unaware of anything or anyone else.'*

When all the infant needs are met and healthy love, eye-contact, joy and engagement are mirrored by mother and other carers, the infant develops a sense that all that she sees and senses when awake is the Universal Potency. As well when sleeping there is also a quiet sensory monitoring that all is well and safe. The infant does not have to 'do' anything. There is no language and therefore no language thought. There is simply experience in the moment and then an invisible, non-painful, neurological processing of all of these events. The brain and the nervous system work together to form memory and reflex as part of survival mechanisms. If there is no threat, there is no direct trauma impact. The experienced sense of omnipotence feels complete and satisfying to the infant.

As we grow the memory/experience-echo of this felt sense of omnipotence permeates the psyche. This is experienced as a longing to return to this state. As life becomes more and more complex there is a strong desire, mostly subconscious, to return to this field of; lack of pain; lack of struggle, void of suffering and without language and therefore thought.

Money within the psyche is imbued with multiple

meanings, experiences and connections. It becomes so complex that truly unravelling or mapping its origins and crisscrossed layers is impossible. It would be like adding millions of shades of colours into a glass of water and then trying to see just one of them. One of the false illusions that money can offer is the feeling of Infantile Omnipotence. Money can symbolise power, worldliness, prestige, control, freedom, security, acceptance and being special — all this combined, even subliminally, feels close to that feeling of being the centre of the Universe. Infantile Omnipotence calls like a siren and the helpless ego structure boards any vessel to get back there. We see money as a great sail-ship mesmerised by the song of the sirens calling it back to Infantile Omnipotence.

Combined with this, the ego structure has an issue with what it perceives as being ordinary. Ordinary feels like the threat of not being seen by the primary care giver (primary wound) and therefore feels like death. We therefore desire a sense of specialness — with money we can buy so many trappings that give the impression that. *'I am special because I have'*. And not the healthy belief that. *'I am special because I am.'*

Money is a symbolic balm against feeling inferior or impotent in life. Money can give those who don't yet have it a false hope, *'When I am rich all this pain and suffering will go away'*. This desperate belief has become pandemic. It is fuelled with celebrity narcissism and enabled with every cellular device.

Anyone who has money will tell you it can't buy true happiness. It can only offer a temporary facsimile. Rich or poor, the same rule applies, know thyself! The only way out is in!

"Our lives are structured around power symbols: money, authority, title, beauty, security."
~ Caroline Myss

We often revert back to our childhood family dynamic — who has power and how can I maintain my share of it, in order to survive. I realise when we are delving into all of this, it appears hopeless. But it isn't, I assure you. We just need to work on what's showing up in the moment with our money issues. We need just one entry point; everyone has at least one.

Money and power issues dwell within us all. They can cause internal conflicts: over dependency and co-dependency; personal responsibility and shared responsibility, individual gains and societal gains. The emotional connotations and triggers stem from our family of origin. The place where we were first imprinted or conditioned by family values, cultural backgrounds, religious doctrine etc. Aspects of the self that are not integrated, and those that are longed for, govern our modus operandi.

The narcissistic need for a perceived completion or wholeness, without self-reflection and self-enquiry (therapy or seeking guidance in self-improvement books, seminars, etc.) leads to a self-governed chaos. In the money wound this manifests in soul harming (peace of mind, ease in life, happiness) behaviours and destructive patterns. Perhaps it won't manifest so dramatically, yet we can be plagued with malaise and a veil of depression. This can all be your money wound obfuscating your true path, purpose and potential.

The attainment of money is one of the most prolific ego ideals. Money is a supreme fuel for narcissistic supply. Basically put, narcissistic supply is the now embedded instinctual need for food (survival) and for omnipotence. As we can't live without money, the **Billionaire Buddha** simply suggests we target our money wound as an inroad to discover, or perhaps more accurately, re-discover, our freedom.

Chapter 5

MONEY & THE WARNING SIGNS

"Money often costs too much."
~ Ralph Waldo Emerson

Here is a comprehensive list, and by no means exhaustive, in ways we are out of integrity with our relationship with money. You may have a similar pattern or a unique one that you could add to this list. It's just a way to get real and honest about how we behave with money. Some acts are small and may seem insignificant and some might be much bigger and a need for concern.

Without judging yourself too harshly or too much self-analysis at this stage, simply make a mental note of some of the things you do on this list. Of course, we will all do a few of these things regardless of our financial status. Even if you only do a few things on the list, you can still benefit enormously from taking emotional responsibility for your actions.

~

Signs of an unhealthy relationship with money — in no particular order. You may have or do the following:

- Incur unsecured debt to make a purchase
- Make major purchases without researching comparative features and prices
- Make major purchases without considering the long-term financial impact
- Watch and buy from a shopping channel
- Shop as a recreational activity
- Spend a lot of time thinking and talking about shopping and the great deals you've gotten
- Own multiple items of essentially the same thing
- Have a closet full of unworn clothing, shelves of unread books, a storage space filled with unused tools, unused hobby equipment, or other unused items
- Rationalise your purchases because you got it second-hand or on sale
- Buy things for other people when you can't rationalise buying them for yourself
- Spend money to please or impress people
- Conceal purchases
- Frequently return purchases
- Feel regret, remorse, guilt or shame after a purchase
- Feel elated after a purchase
- Feel down after a shopping trip has ended
- Shop to cheer yourself up
- Shop to calm yourself down

- Lack money to pay for basics after purchasing less essential items
- Have a spouse, parent or child who criticises or worries about your spending
- Have friends or family who joke about your spending habits
- Neglected basic responsibilities because of time spent shopping
- Stolen items whether or not you had the money to buy them
- Believe that a given purchase would fix some aspect of your life
- Lost a relationship or job because of your spending
- Resent a low pay or bad job situation, yet not asking for a raise or changing jobs
- Feeling inadequate to perform a job well, while secretly feeling superior to others
- Believing your salary is not important, yet worrying about money constantly
- Feeling too discouraged to apply for a job. (*'I won't get it anyway, and if I do, I'll hate it.'*)
- Having trouble finding resumes or job notices in piles of bills or unopened mail
- Feeling ashamed of your work history and sick with anxiety over job interviews
- Stealing from employers because you believe they owe you more than they pay you
- Spending hours daydreaming but not even minutes working toward your dreams
- Over committing time and energy to volunteer activities
- Overworking-spending hours to do a job more perfectly than you are getting paid to do
- Being too fearful of failure to get any more training or

attempt a new career

- Believing no one will pay you for anything you enjoy doing
- Being unclear about your financial situation
- Not knowing account balances, monthly expenses, loan interest rates, fees, fines, or contractual obligations
- Frequently *'borrowing'* items such as books, pens, or small amounts of money from friends and others, and failing to return them
- Poor saving habits
- Not planning for taxes, retirement or other not-recurring but predictable items, and then feeling surprised when they come in; a *'live for today, don't worry about tomorrow'* attitude
- Compulsive shopping: Being unable to pass up a *'good deal'*, making impulsive purchases; leaving price tags on clothes so they can be returned; not using items you've purchased
- Difficulty in meeting basic financial or personal obligations, and/or an excessive sense of accomplishment when such obligations are met
- A different feeling when buying things on credit than when paying cash, a feeling of being in the club, of being accepted, of being grown up
- Living in chaos and drama around money
- Using one credit card to pay another
- Bouncing cheques
- Always having a financial crisis to contend with
- A tendency to live on the edge
- Living paycheque to paycheque
- Taking risks with health and car insurance coverage
- Writing cheques hoping money will appear to cover them
- Unwarranted inhibition and embarrassment in what

should be a normal discussion of money
- Overworking or underearning
- Working extra hours to earn money to pay creditors
- Using time inefficiently
- Taking jobs below your skill and education level
- An unwillingness to care for and value yourself
- Living in self-imposed deprivation
- Denying your basic needs in order to pay your creditors
- A feast or famine mentality
- A feeling or hope that someone will take care of you if necessary, so that you won't really get into serious financial trouble, that there will always be someone you can turn to.

Chapter 6

MONEY & THE SABOTEUR

*"Our inner beliefs trigger failure before it happens.
They sabotage lasting change by cancelling its
possibility."* ~ Marshall Goldsmith

The word saboteur or sabotage was linked to French cottage workers in the industrial revolution protesting the progress of automation of their industries, as a threat to their livelihoods and incomes. They threw sabots (wooden clogs) into the new machines to try and break them and halt progress.

Our society as it is today only functions with money. So, it makes sense to choose an easy and productive relationship with it. No one in their right mind would want to sabotage that necessary flow to make all the twists and turns of life a little more bearable, would they? Yet, we are all interrupting this flow somehow. Most of us are familiar with this character in our lives who takes us down the wrong path despite all our best intentions and wisdom.

The Saboteur is that wilful character trait that defies all logic and perversely obstructs your good life. It hijacks you by emotional and psychological patterning and behaviour before you apparently have any choice in the matter. It is the force in your life, if kept in check, can help you move from **Blindful** to **Mindful**.

Carl Jung suggested we are influenced by powerful psychological patterns which he personified into Archetypes. Archetypes are a great way to put some distance between you and the problem. It's often easier to work out how the archetype is sabotaging our lives rather than beat ourselves up at our own failings. It's a tried and tested therapeutic device that works. We tend to see ourselves strongly in one archetype, possibly two. And we will have characteristics from all of them in varying quantities.

Archetypes stem from ancient and universal human qualities and ways of being that are integrated into our individual psyche and behaviour. The Saboteur is one of the many archetypes we play out in our life. The great medical intuitive and mystic, Caroline Myss describes The Saboteur as being '*... made up of the fears and issues related to low self-esteem that cause you to make choices in life that block your own empowerment and success*'.

When unchecked in our financial lives the Saboteur forms self-destructive behaviours: bad financial decisions, unconsciously losing money, overspending and taking risks with our hard-earned cash without ever doing extensive due-diligence. The Saboteur adds stress and a disconnection from the sense of a benevolent universe that keeps us in grace and flow.

If we make friends with The Saboteur, we can learn a lot about our habitual dysfunction and get on with healing a path towards financial stability and freedom. When we identify how we sabotage ourselves, particularly in regard to our finances, we start to realise our greatest potential and transform our lives.

Further along in the book we will look at Money Masks; some of the different archetypes we operate under that affect our relationship with money. The Money Mask archetype called the Financial Saboteur has such a painful and corrosive effect on our lives that it deserved a complete chapter.

So how does the Financial Saboteur show up in our lives? This list is many and varied, for example, it is when we feel incapable of lifting ourselves to a higher pay bracket. When we believe that we must stick to a job we hate rather than managing ourselves into a position we may love. When we do not do due diligence on investments or loans and put our hard-earned money at risk. It can also be when we don't take measured risk to advance our financial position and security. The Financial Saboteur is there when we are unable to act on economic opportunities that fall in our path because we just don't have the spare cash to get in on the game. It is present when we allow our credit card debt to become unmanageable. When we under earn, which in turn profoundly effects our sense of worth.

These are just some of the ways the Financial Saboteur is at play in our financial lives and the list of its influence by no means ends there.

The Financial Saboteur also works macrocosmically in humanity. Consider how we have designed an economic structure that says in many instances, *'for some to profit, others must suffer.'* This inevitably cultivates a win/lose rather than a win/win in many economic situations across the world. The macrocosmic Financial Saboteur is there when choices are made that cost people their livelihoods, screw down wages for profit, have detrimental impact on the environment or has workers in substandard or even dangerous working conditions to improve the bottom line. As we have seen from recent history, we have come a long way. And yet we are far from the ideal. There is only one way to change the collective psyche and that is to have enough individuals working on their own psyche to enable sufficient change. In essence it's the hundredth monkey effect.

The hundredth monkey effect is a hypothetical phenomenon in which a new behaviour or idea is claimed to spread rapidly by unexplained means from one group to all related groups once a critical number of members of one group exhibit the new behaviour or acknowledge the new idea. *The Billionaire Buddha* is asking you to be part of the global change by simply getting a handle on your finances, being mindful of your financial wounds and gaining a sense of peace.

It's challenging when I work with clients who are divorcing, and both have their Financial Saboteurs running the show. Invariably, both clients are compromised with regards to their financial outcomes and for their solicitors … well their own Financial Saboteur is rubbing their hands together! Usually, I am working with one side of the party and I have seen examples where my client, who's in such emotional collapse, (which is understandable) walks away from financial settlements with less than what is reasonable. I often work with only one side, which I am seeking to change. I believe working with both sides in a financial divorce settlement would be a lot more helpful and healing for both parties. As Gwyneth Paltrow coined in her own separation from Chris Martin, a 'conscious uncoupling,' particularly in relation to a fair and equal financial settlement.

Again, I want to motivate you into this enquiry. I know if you're new to all of this it might feel too hard. Especially if you are in the middle of a downward emotional spiral. I understand it. Please don't give up hope. You can do this … I promise you after the emotional mining you will find your pot of gold. Except this time, it won't be at the end of a rainbow. It will be in your self-worth and your net-worth. I love the following quote as it asks us to change our perspective on the way we go about a dilemma.

"Your task is not to seek for love, but merely to seek and find all the barriers within yourself that you have built against it." ~ Rumi

That's what you are doing here at *The Billionaire Buddha*. Your goal hasn't wavered, but your strategy and perspective have. Keep working through the *28 Day Challenge* and stay curious about what you find.

What makes up our own individual Financial Saboteur is all the fears and challenges we have about money. Where we may have aspects of low self-esteem and how we then project this on to our relationship with money. We unconsciously block money, empowerment and opportunity in our life because of our deeper issues of lack of self-esteem. When we continue to ignore our deeper issues, the Financial Saboteur will operate on our behalf, making disastrous financial decisions for us. When we discover some of these deeper issues, we can reduce the influence of the Financial Saboteur. More often than not, how we deal with money is how we deal with ourselves: **If you respect yourself, you will respect money: If you respect money, you will respect yourself.**

Chapter 7

THE MONEY WOUND

"Through money or power, you cannot solve all problems. The problem in the human heart must be solved first." ~ Dalai Lama

ден

Sigmund Freud postulated that our thoughts and actions as adults have their source in our early infancy and childhood. This is unconscious in our psyche and directs our behaviour as adults. By unconscious I mean we don't readily see or experience the motivation for our responses to life. It's a bit like the difference between manually flying a plane and auto-pilot. The conscious pilot knows what he is doing and makes rational decisions based on facts. The unconscious is our auto-pilot basing decisions on old programming ... based on an old wounding.

We all operate from our wounds. This means that all the experiences we have ever had — painful, traumatic or shocking, in some way cloud or muddy our thoughts, actions and reactions in the present moment. Of course, this is true of positive experience too. But it's the negative experiences that often shape our fear, protection and defence around survival. These now engrained strategies and beliefs forge our personalities and behaviours. Trouble is they are often outdated and no longer serve us. Yet the core wound still broadcasts a warning echo and the part of us that is responsible for our survival goes on automatic pilot. Obviously, I am simplifying it here and there is more and more research into this field augmenting the research and theory based on the Freudian concepts of Self, the Id, Ego, Dreams etc.

Without doing some form of personal development work to identify and hopefully heal some of our wounds, we may never be free of our repetitive fixations, beliefs and behaviours. So not surprisingly we bring our wounds from the past about money into all and every aspect of our daily life. As such, we all operate from our *money wounds*. You could say that a bank robber has been completely hijacked by his *money wound*.

Another name for the *money wound* would be the *survival wound*. All the issues or challenges we experience with our need to survive, i.e. provide for ourselves and work within a communal fiscal system; food, shelter, clothing surmounts to our day to day bodily survival. It is what we do every day to essentially keep ourselves alive, or metaphorically, to put bread on our table. We all have the same task and yet we all have individual psychological issues and challenges which determine how we execute this process of taking care of ourselves. Our *money wounds* are entirely unique.

Our *money wound* shows up when we can't afford to buy that car we want or even fix the one we have. When we have sleepless nights thinking about those mortgage repayments or the big deal we are trying to pull off at work. It shows up when we discover our bank balance is getting low or when we have gone a little crazy on our credit cards. Imagine your *money wound* is at the centre of a giant spider's web. No matter where the web is touched, it will always reverberate into the centre. Think of your *money wound* as a big preying spider.

Whole communities have *money wounds*. Just look at what can happen when a corporation pushes out indigenous people for profit or communities fight to stop coal seam drilling. Even nations can have *money wounds*. The most recent and poignant examples of Greece and Spain's economic woes, two nations in the grip of their own collective *money wounds*.

Our *money wound* also shows up in how we relate to others when we undervalue ourselves or when we withhold money as a form of power. It shows up when we use money to feel superior. Or when we get angry at those who have more than us and take some judgemental moral high ground discussing our coveting desires.

Our *money wounds* are everywhere, they are complex and mostly hidden from our conscious mind and can sometimes hijack us apparently out of nowhere, setting our nerves on end and peace of mind nowhere to be found.

Our drive to get money, make money and even push money away has its source in our *money wound*. The lower income brackets operate from their *money wounds* and it is felt in their heads, hearts and stomachs. Every wealthy person on the planet is governed by this early programming. Even money or success gurus, like Anthony Robbins, are acting out their *money wounds*. These people can often articulate their *money wounds* and use it in their narratives of how they became wealthy. If they had experiences of feeling insignificant, they may use the accumulation of wealth to achieve significance. If they were a complete disaster with money, their wound may inspire them to become a master of money. If they went hungry as children, they might vow to never go hungry again.

Even the noblest acts of generosity have a thread of the wound at their source either from early childhood or from the accumulated experiences as an adult. The difference between a judgement or an observation is that an observation has no emotional weight or charge. I am trying to be objective here, without judgement, in order to illustrate that none of us are exempt from having our wounds drive our behaviour with money.

My care as a Financial Therapist is borne out of my own *money wound*. Knowing how intimately flawed and painful my relationship was with money, I have a drive to help others heal their money stories.

"Human happiness and human satisfaction must ultimately come from within oneself. It is wrong to expect some final satisfaction to come from money or from a computer." ~ Dalai Lama

The greatest mystery in the universe over any scientific discovery, new frontier or far off distant galaxy, is the mystery of the self. We are such complex, confusing, contradictory and utterly mysterious creatures. At any moment, our reaction to something good or bad will have its trigger in some far-off distant memory or recent experience.

We of course would go mad if all our unconscious urges and impulses were made conscious and had a 'voice'. In therapy we slowly excavate into the core of a wound only when there are obvious breakdowns in function: dysfunction. We go mining when something is so broken that we must dig deep to find the cause and then gingerly find a remedy. We have to pick our battles. But as money is woven through every aspect of our lives, I believe it's one of the best battles to conquer.

It would be naive to assume that there is a direct tunnel into a wound. It is always a complex 3D matrix (with the odd wormhole thrown in). Most of the time we will be unaware of the definitive origin of our reactivity in a single situation. Our mind may project a possibility of its source. However, the particulars of a present reaction to a specific event is diffused with a thousand plus nuances from many different past experiences. We could never say with absolute certainty that we do x because y happened to us when we were six years old. And yet, we have to start somewhere.

I ask my clients to trust the process and to trust their senses — how it actually feels in their bodies. This sensory-barometer will always point us in the right direction. We can slowly get the gist of why we do and act the way we do — especially if we have recurring patterns or dysfunctions.

With this in mind, you can appreciate how tricky it is to truly understand our *money wound*. It will always be a work in progress. Perhaps not always linear but hopefully always tracking forward and the road should get more and more comfortable the more we push on.

We are continually in a non-static relationship with money. We are relating to money in either positive, neutral, or highly charged ways every single day. We never get any time off, ever! Whether we like it or not ... we cannot be in this modern world without money. Even those who attempt to live 'off grid' need the tangible coin at some point.

It's not that we are all obsessed with money. It's simply the evolution of our materialistic and consumerist society that in the modern world we cannot function without it. We think about money and transactions many times an hour: buying our morning coffee, going into work to pay the bills, paying bills, deciding whether we can afford that holiday, finding money in the street, working so our business stays afloat, checking our bank balance daily (some people hourly). At some level an emotional response will be present in all of these actions or reflections. All interactions are showing something about your relationship with money. This makes pinning down the slippery *money wound* even more difficult.

Just like our relationship with the ones we love, our relationship with money and dealing with our *money wounds* can sometimes drive us a little crazy.

Recognising that we all have *money wounds* (except the Dalai Lama and The Queen — neither carry nor use money) is a great start.

Recognising how much time you dedicate to thinking, worrying and dealing with money is a poignant illustration at how significant this relationship is. It's a relationship worth analysing. Think of all the wonderful things you could be doing with that time and energy ... mostly resting, having fun or perhaps making even more money!

~

In the mid-nineties I studied with the eminent Chilean psychiatrist Claudio Naranjo. He is one of three successors of Fritz Perls, the founder of world-renowned Gestalt Therapy. Gestalt Therapy was a theory and practice developed in some way in direct response to Freudian psychoanalysis. It is a relational therapy as opposed to an analytical therapy. Naranjo was a student of the great philosopher Oscar Ichazo. Naranjo is also recognised as one of the principal developers and teachers of the nine personality types illustrated in the *Enneagram* of Personality (*Enneagram*) theory.

The *Enneagram* is a mapping of nine different personality types or psychological fixations that emerge to compensate for the loss of unconditional love, trust and security in our relationship with life and living. We use these psychological or emotional regulation strategies as thought and behavioural patterns that try to fix our wounds and make things right in our life. It shows us how our survival mechanism rules us in unconscious ways that cause us to suffer. The system helps us explore how we became attached and identified with these patterns. How we identify more so with one of the nine and then explore the nuances within each personality type. We discover the ego identity that dictates who we *think* we are. The *Enneagram* points to why we are run by patterns and what we are truly seeking. It gives us sensitive discernment to what runs us behaviourally.

In our development from new-born to adult we gradually lose our essential or fundamental essence. Essence here is described as that presence, passion and security we are born with. The unique talents and qualities that are inexplicably 'us'. It is not a question of nature or nurture. Some people are funny, studious, musical, altruistic, curious etc. Our essence is our very own unique colour or flavour and can be characterised by qualities such innate confidence, internal strength and a sense of powerfulness and joy. In the unfoldment of life, we become fixated by the past or future, rather than trusting in the all-encompassing Now. We lose touch with our essential qualities or at best we are too afraid to trust them. Freud called this essential nature the Id. The moments before our ego structure forms. The ego structure modifies our behaviour to enable us to get up, get over or get along in life in either positive or negative ways.

In *Enneagram* terms this ego structure has nine different thought and behaviour pattern types. They all have both strengths (integrated states) and weaknesses (disintegrated states). These are traits that we can either see ourselves or other people can readily see in us. And within all of this there are blind spots. These thoughts and behaviour types are borne from specific types of experiences in our childhood that lay down different ways of perceiving the world, depending on the environment in which we were raised.

The following *Enneagram* Types (Enneatypes) illustrate firstly the environment the infant was born into and is expressed here as the 'Attachment Style'. And secondly the 'World View', the childhood that was later internalised and colours us as adults. Like everything, there is a spectrum. Our childhoods may have been completely idyllic or traumatic. Some readers may believe that their childhood was idyllic, and with a distant wide lens they probably were. But let us remember there were many moments (or hours, days, weeks or even months) in our childhood where our needs and desires were not being met, either reasonably or unreasonably. What we are looking for here is how our care givers reacted to our expectations. Our care givers over those many years may have been; unwell, distracted, traumatised, absent, present sometimes and gone the next. And there we are; wanting, needing, wanting and needing. This basic survival interaction constructs our generalised and specific world view. When we are growing our neural pathways form physically and are then reflected in fixations, personality and behaviour. The progressive speed that a baby processes life and forms and connects neural pathways is astonishing.

The Attachment Style, the style in which we attached to our care giver as a mechanism for survival, led to the construction of our ego structure or ego strategies. Dr Allan Schore, the American psychologist and researcher in the area of neuropsychology believes that 90% of our adult relating to the world comes from our initial Attachment Style or Attachment Relationship.

This becomes challenging, even deeply

problematic, if this initial relationship was not very secure or supportive. The good news is most practitioners in the neuro-psychology and somatic-psychology field believe that with self-enquiry our neuro-plasticity can change to build a healthier and more secure relationship both with ourselves and the world around us. In short, we can move from mild to severe dysfunction into a functional and integrated human being.

What does this mean when we want to be more than just a functional human being? When we want to thrive, rather than just survive? How can we shine some light on some of our own blindspots? Particularly in relationship with money. The *money wound* is so intrinsically linked to our survival and has its origins in our Attachment Relationship. In looking at our *money wounds* we are effectively killing two birds with one stone. We attempt to improve our financial status and our overall relationship with Life.

Through the lens of the *Enneagram* we can gain insights about our thought and behavioural patterns. I have found it particularly efficient in mine and my clients' relationship with money. In the following Enneatype descriptions, you will notice, I have deliberately focused on the negative fixations and behavioural patterns as a way, to shock, shake up and crack into your conditioned structure.

The goal of *The Billionaire Buddha* is to help us to get closer or return to that essential state where unconditional love, trust and security abides. In putting our relationship with money under the microscope we can discover multiple layers of personality mapping or programming. Our aim is always to do life better.

The internet will give you bountiful information on what *Enneagram* Type you may be. Some teachers have a personal growth angle, and some have a more spiritual bent. See what works for you! For the purposes of healing our *money wound*, we will explore how each Enneatype relates to money. Remember this is simply a tool of self-enquiry. It is not a diagnostic tool that keeps you locked in a disintegrated pattern. It is a tool to excavate your true whole and healthy Essence — those qualities can never be altered. They dwell within you, perhaps shrouded in veils. Nevertheless they are there, intact and waiting to re-write the stuck or stale programming of your life. If we operate from a deep sense of knowing, trusting, loving security … our whole lives leap from black and white to technicolour.

"The wound is the place where the light enters you"
~ Rumi

ден

i

Type One

If I am perfect, I will receive money (Love/Trust/Security)

Attachment Style: The source of care (mostly mother in infancy) is either highly critical, rejecting or withholding with an expectation for the infant to be of a certain 'standard'. For example; the carer's need for something from the child, to be perfectly behaved for example, perhaps to be more like a friend or sibling, or for the child to take care of the carer in the 'right way' … to behave in a way that fulfils the carer's expectations. If those expectations are not met, then the biological needs of the child are threatened or at least reluctantly met.

World View: The *money wound* Type One has internalised the care giver's need for this standard into a belief that will return the Type One to a perceived sense of 'essential perfection'. *If I meet my carer's expectations, if I am good and perfect, I will be worthy of survival.'* With this belief system, all survival and financial reward will be integrated *only* when Type Ones can be, do and act according to an internalised drive to reach the prescribed standard of perfection dictated by the carer. Of course, this is never achievable. The echoes of this reverberate into adult life and shadow all relationships.

Self-control and self-regulation are the modus operandi when dealing with money for Type Ones. Being both risk adverse and rigidly conservative. Type Ones are meticulous with their management of money and are diligent budgeters. The obsessive need to be a perfect money manager can be a way of compensating for their lack of 'essential perfection'.

Type One's relationship with money can appear rigid. They opt for a secure pay packet over 'risking it all to follow their dreams.' Following their dreams may cause them to unravel a little as they move outside of their comfort zone. In extreme cases unfulfilled lives and bitter unhappiness are the sacrifice for stability and survival.

Type Ones limit their beliefs about a future potential to earn more, rather accepting that what they earn is measured outside of them, not internally. They have many money rules, such as, restraint and conservative spending, which are vital in dealing with money.

Of course, a measured and realistic approach to spending is wise but not at the cost of squeezing out the spontaneity and playfulness money can bring.

When Type Ones are under financial stress their drive for perfection is turned inward and negative self-talk can escalate. They also become highly critical of other people's management of funds. Their untamed judgements can alienate them from friends and family. They become righteous and are caught in the lie that if they don't reach this standard (now an invisible wound) that their needs will not be met.

All this pressure can motivate in a negative way or entirely demotivate their ability to financially survive, do well or thrive. Wealth and Success are measured through an internalised mechanism that has little to do with their innate self-worth, innate self-value or ability to just Be in the world — their essential qualities; their true essence.

Money Mask: The earning and receiving of money is done with a strict self-modulated structure of 'acting perfect' for the right results and for approval and acceptance. This masks their fundamental flaw of a sense of lacking the 'right' stuff or essential perfection for survival.

Money Meditation: Contemplating that there is something truly perfect in all our flaws and failings is an entry point for Type Ones towards relaxation and healing. When the need to be perfect, or the inner and outward mealy-mouthed judge shows up, this is the time to remind a Type One to stop, reflect and meditate on the source of their maddening beliefs. Kind self-enquiry with a reputable therapist would be very useful. With the goal of getting brave to be a little messy, (maybe just for a little while!).

Money Wound Antidote: I am essentially perfect

just as I am, with and without material gains.

ii

Type Two

**_If I am giving and kind, I will receive money
(Love/Trust/Security)_**

Attachment Style: The source of care was needy, wilful, the centre of attention or commanded more attention than the needs of the infant. To meet their biological needs Type Twos had to subvert their own impulses. Instead they set to the task of manipulation and timing to capture the focus of the care giver. They abandon their own needs and focussed on the needs of the other.

World View: The Enneatype Two's Attachment Relationship has internalised the principle: *'If I place my own needs behind the needs of others, I will receive the pot of gold.'* Setting this as their constant course means the Type Two can never land in their own innate path. The road to riches is conditioned, they must capture the leprechaun first. This builds as resentment and disdain in Type Two. They are not free to be themselves with their needs. They have lost their 'essential freedom'. They ache under the reality that life seems to support everyone else but them. Therefore, they resolve to lock on and manipulate others using the device of being giving and indispensable as a strategy to increase their importance.

A classic Type Two is the 'woman behind the man'. She is excessively ardent, adoring and builds indispensability as a strategy for her survival and fortune. Type Twos find it almost impossible to ask for more on their own merits. Their internal landscape is featureless, flat, without any value, so they feel they are not deserving. Giving, generosity and being selfless to others is not done as a noble act, but rather a tactic to get more (to get love, trust and security). You will find a large volume of Type Twos in a celebrity entourage. The archetypical desire for a sugar daddy or to be rescued is typical of this type.

Type Twos are impulsive buyers, lack financial restraint, and are commonly excessive retail shoppers with expensive tastes. Their consumption is limitless, which shows in their credit cards being often over the limit. Money can be a tool for buying love. The Type Two acts as a benevolent ornate cornucopia that is usually empty.

Under financial stress Type Twos can be vindictive and revengeful, taking other parties to the cleaners. When financial reward is not forthcoming, they turn to guilt tripping, sending an invoice showing of all their benevolence as proof of their need to be paid, plus interest!

Money Mask: Naranjo called a Type Two's mask 'False Humility'. A self-sacrificing seducer that covers their own torturous neediness. Their need to indulge materialistically tries to fill the deprived vacuum that left a void as an infant.

Money Meditation: You are the centre of the universe. The belief that everything you need can only come from another is just that, a belief. When you finally give to yourself you will realise it is more nourishing, more beautiful and more precious than any gift that anyone can give to you.

Money Wound Antidote: Giving to myself will set me free. Self-care. Self-love. Self-respect. When I give, I will give from a full cup. I will give freely when I myself am nourished.

iii

Type Three

**If I am striving, I will receive money
(Love/Trust/Security)**

Attachment Style: The source of care was stretched, overburdened, neglectful or absent. The Three took over the role of care giver to themselves. Building self-sufficiency for their biological needs, *'My care giver is not here; I will have to do it all for myself.'*

World View: It is as though an infant Type Three is waiting for their dinner, but no-one is home, so decides to climb down from the highchair to cook their own meal. *'Life will not give me what I need, so I need to create it myself'.* They have lost the 'essential faith' that life will support and sustain them. They do not believe a benevolent source will dole things out to them, so they become god-like unto themselves. *'I am the source of creation in my world — I cannot rely on anyone but myself.'* In extreme disintegration Type Threes develop a personality psyche akin to God itself. We see this often reflected in the collective consciousness which values and reveres wealthy people as god-like, more superior somehow, than the rest of us.

The image of Type Three is all that matters. The outward bravado of success and how they appear to others is vital in the receiving and accumulation of money. Type Threes build an image of trust and confidence in the mind of the buyer (friend, partner, spouse), rather than an innate sense of value, trust and confidence coming from within. They can lacquer themselves in any veneer required for the transaction. They become a chameleon; to one client the hapless salesman, to the next, a sleek professional. They exude a false empathy that helps people remember them. They are magicians and masters of disguise. A classic Type Three is the clichéd car salesman who changes his personality seamlessly depending on the buyer.

Their mercilessness and cold-steel determination in the accumulation of money costs them their health and personal relationships. The Type Three is the classic absent father who worked tirelessly on his business for years on end. Only to regretfully wish on his death bed he had spent more time with his kids. Or the lone woman in a 'man's world' trying to crack the glass ceiling at the cost of having no children of her own.

Money Mask: Appearance is more important than substance. They are the quintessential snake oil seller or Svengali. The Type Three structure covers an aching mournfulness that no-one is truly there for them. The phrase *'If I am seen more or have more showy wealth, I will receive more love.'* hits at the heart of every achievement or success.

Money Meditation: Nature and the abundance it generously provides helps reflect the benevolence of this world. Breathe deeply and slowly ... practice stillness and gratitude for all that money cannot buy. Between the in and the out breath there is a sustaining silence. Every breathe we take, is a simple yet exquisite reminder that life sustains us. Profoundly understanding this is the most successful achievement. That I am supported in just Being without the Doing.

Money Wound Antidote: I am enough for myself. Just opening my eyes in the morning is enough. Standing naked without my material wealth and developing trust; trust in others coupled with asking for emotional support will help me break the belief that I have to do it alone. Being seen as authentic, honest and vulnerable will bring meaningful relationships closer to me. Collaboration brings connection.

iv

Type Four

If I long and yearn, I will receive money (Love/Trust/Security)

Attachment Style: The source of care was disengaged, absent or withdrawn. In the extreme, the infant was completely abandoned. The biological needs were met with a sense of neglect, being forgotten and overlooked or catastrophically forsaken.

World View: *'The world doesn't want me; I am alone and disconnected from the source of all that will sustain me.'* Type Fours have lost contact with the 'essential oneness' or interconnectedness of life. They feel alone and a distinct separation from the flow of an abundant life. This sets their personality structure into longing and yearning that can present to the world as being needy, poor me or helpless me. The tinge of the world owes me, and victimhood are prevalent. Type Fours are the quintessential poor suffering artist. They use money as a tool for creative or emotional catharsis of their longing. Longing for money is more important than receiving it. Which means even if they are financially stable, with dollars in the bank, they somehow still feel that they fall short. There is a gaping hole desperate to be filled.

Under financial stress Type Fours collapse, can become lost, catastrophise and ineffectual in their own recovery; needing to be bailed out or go into bankruptcy. Attempting to teach or assist Type Fours with financial efficacy will be met with a structure that says, *'Money gets in the way of my process'* or *'Can someone else manage this money thing for me?'*

Of all the Enneatypes, the Four has a sense of scarcity as their modus operandi. Bringing a meagreness and inner poverty consciousness to their world. This leads the Type Four to believe they are somehow deficient and inadequate to deal with money.

Money Mask: Type Fours use their artistic or a *poor me* mask to gain sympathy or financial support. This is garnered by an entitlement that they suffer more than everyone else, so they deserve it more. It is true, they do feel more profoundly than the rest of us. Their primary relationship has left them eternally grieving and where other Enneatypes' masks provide false relief, for the Four their apparent payoff comes if they wear their initial wound on the sleeve for all to see.

Money Meditation: Quantum physics teaches us

that there is no separation in the universe. We are all inexplicably part of the whole, of oneness. It is only the personality structure, the core wounds of the ego, that believes we are separate. The journey back from perceived separation to oneness is through the heart. Type Fours know the inner chambers of the heart for emotional suffering. They need to find the doorways of inner joy, creativity and connectedness. If Type Fours can conquer their finances ... they can utilise their talents more effectively as true gifts to the world.

Money Wound Antidote: I am connected to all of life. All that I am longing for is within my reach. Gratitude for all that I bring to the world will help reflect just how connected I am. I am not alone. In truly helping myself I can enjoy authentic feelings of fullness, wholeness and oneness. Acknowledging all that life has already given me will build trust and safety. Sharing good news about my fortunes, great and small, endear people towards me. I have a sacred obligation to take care of myself with love, kindness and compassion.

v

Type Five

If I am knowing, I will receive money (Love/Trust/Security)

Attachment Style: The source of care was either intrusive, smothering or invasive; or conversely aloof. Or the child's unique needs were unknown by the care giver and not really understood. The biological needs were met with a lack of knowing the intrinsic needs and desires of the infant. The care giver was more concerned with their own needs, exclusive of the needs of the child.

World View: *'My intrinsic needs and desires were never seen or more importantly known by my care giver, as though I were invisible.'* Painfully for the Type Five, the structure of being invisible triggers the primary wound — *'If you don't see me, you will not feed me?'* From this question, from the pit of their belly they are thrust to the edge of the existential vacuum, *'If I am not seen, not known as my intrinsic self...will I exist?'* Fearing for their life, the Type Five moves to the mind. *'The world doesn't see me, doesn't know me, I need to know why.'* They have lost touch with the 'essential knowing'. The greatest knowing (the knowing that we all really don't know), seems to hit this type more squarely in the back pocket than any other Enneatypes. This gives them a keen mind and a sharp intellect. They feel safe with knowledge; safe within the mind.

With their great minds, Type Fives have a personality structure that knows they are utilitarian in the market, so may not be as outwardly challenged as other Enneatypes are with money. Type Fives are often sensitive and may feel that their usefulness in the market locks them into analytical careers. Often, they wish for something a little more adventurous but cannot take the risk of the unknown. The Monty Python sketch of the accountant wanting to become a lion tamer humorously illustrates this point.

Under financial stress Type Fives become staunchly methodical, crunching numbers and searching for the unknown factor that will give them that edge. The mind kicks in needing to extensively research, over analyse and calculate risk ad infinitum. You might guess, economists, financial analysts, actuaries and treasurers are most probably Type Five.

Money Mask: It is crazy to think that heads of National Reserves, Government Treasuries, the IMF and major banks around the world are suffering from an existential need to be truly, deeply, profoundly seen and known. Being in the mind, keeps Type Fives away from that terrifying pit. Data, figures, numbers and models help to busy this type. They have no time for contemplating another person's strategies. For them this risks annihilation. Their usefulness in the market can be a mask for them to not be *really* seen and understood as themselves: who they truly are. Type Fives will survive financially but at the cost of no-one essentially knowing the great mystery of who they are.

Money Meditation: The highest forms of mathematics seek to deconstruct the most mysterious; God if you will. That is all very well, but let the world see and know the mysteriousness in you. Let your brilliant mind have the honest luxury of, *Know Thyself.* No matter how much this journey will take you into the unknown territories of the senses … it will also free your mind for fun, spontaneity and hedonistic delights.

Money Wound Antidote: I have a divine birth right to experience my whole sensory body and find pleasure and safety in that. I will be gentle with myself and experiment with taking risks and being spontaneous. Small steps out of my safety zone will be good for me. I will be seen, appreciated and even loved for who I am and not just for what I can do. I will self-enquire around qualities of Being whilst I explore the unknown.

Type Six

**If I am loyal or the opposite, a rebel, I will receive
money (Love/Trust/Security)**

Attachment Style: The source of care was erratic,
untrustworthy, unpredictable or the caregiver felt ill
equipped or highly insecure for the task of parenting. The
biological needs were met with an anticipation of possible
trauma or a wide variation in the quality of care.

World View: The world cannot be fully trusted by
the Type Six, which they hold in their psyche as a loss of
'essential trust' and 'essential strength'. With the loss of
both internal strength and faith, they move outwards,
hitching their wagon to other's authoritative financial
visions, rather than serving their core happiness and
financial efficacy.

Type Six has two contrary forces from the loss of internal strength. Firstly, a need to find strength from without, being loyal to any authoritative external source to compensate for the perceived loss of 'essential strength'. Secondly, a fearing or questioning of the authoritative external source, which reflects painful memories of the early attachment environment.

As with many aspects of a Type Six's life, they can be riddled with doubt, lack of confidence and have suspicions about dealing with money and financial affairs. As such, they tend to be confused around large financial decisions oscillating from what they have garnered from authoritative financial sources and at the same time mistrusting that same source.

Under financial stress Type Six can become paranoid and flooded with feelings of a lack of security and fear. They can appear confused and have a heightened urgency for a need to know all perspectives and realities. Their suspicions can fill in the gaps which adds to their paranoia when they become truly disintegrated. They can be physically agitated and are prone to anxiety and insomnia.

Money Mask: To avert any potential of excruciating anxiety, from possible threat at any moment held in their psyche, Type Six wear their Money Mask with a flavour of cynicism or straight out rebellion. From money not having any importance in life (over spiritualising), to generalised belief systems; *'All rich people are greedy'* or *'I am just not worth that much.'* This is a strategy to avoid the first wound, that life is unpredictable and possibly unsafe, so the Type Six sets about making assumption about the inner and outer world, as a form of protection.

At their most extreme the Six that rebels can justify financial criminality for a noble cause, playing Robyn Hood. Conversely, they can gravitate toward a monastic life (without desire) as is often seen in spiritual circles. Often the Six with a rebel heart can oscillate between renouncing material gain and panicking without it for worry about the future.

Money Meditation: Nature with its contractions and expansions, predictability and chaos, as a source that sustains us in life here on Earth, speaks to the essential trust, beyond the constructs of the paranoid, fearing mind. This vitally volatile and valuable environment can teach us to relax, centre and trust any amount of change. Nature will give you trust, in bucket loads.

Money Wound Antidote: I recognise that the only constant is change. I will spend time in nature and witness the inevitability of the cycles of life. I trust that after the storm will come the calm. And after the calm there will come a storm. Nature grounds me and reminds me that I cannot predict everything, and I don't need to know what is coming in order to feel safe and secure. I recognise that letting go of the need to know and predict outcomes, is all I need to be with. I will converse with nature and listen intently for the innate wisdom she freely shares. I will find ways to self-soothe, self-regulate in a constant way that regulates my nervous system.

vii

Type Seven

**If I constantly seek, I will receive money
(Love/Trust/Security)**

Attachment Style: The source of care either lacked the blissful union of unconditional carer and infant bonding or the blissful union was present, but suddenly stopped or was interrupted, often abruptly. The biological needs were met but there was no expansive love. Perhaps there was nourishment that nourished the body, but not the soul.

World View: Life is a barren wasteland. *'As this is too unbearable to bare, I will seek and dream up plans to get me the hell out of here!'* Type Sevens are the hustlers, dreamers and wranglers of the Enneagram. Gamblers and at their most extreme, bank robbers and con men at their very worst.

They have lost a sense of safety with the 'essential blueprint'. The blueprint that life is a perfectly and intricately designed unknowable unfoldment. Type Sevens take it upon themselves to rustle up a plan to avoid that unknowable unfoldment which to them feels like a parched desert. They are pleasure seekers and their motivation for earning and receiving money is to buy that mythical balm to heal the pain that sits constantly within their psyche.

They are big spenders, bad savers, and will have many jobs, careers and businesses over their lifetime. They are likely to experience many moments of financial insecurity, due to their inability to stay, when the real work needs to be done to create financial security. This can be torturous for the Type Sevens especially as they get older. Not knowing where the next paycheck will come from means they can't buy that ticket out of here. Conversely the contemplation of staying, doing the hard slog may mean there will be little pleasure or the missed opportunity for bigger and better things — so they are exquisitely trapped.

Type Sevens are completely geared for pain avoidance. Yet their behaviour as gamblers, lottery ticket hopefuls and frequent participators in the next big thing without proper due diligence means they often find themselves in a financial wilderness ... and pain.

Money Mask: Considering their internal landscapes, Type Sevens appear to be financial optimists. This optimism and positivity about financial undertakings is a true mask, that covers their core belief — that paradise is lost. They are the clowns with the painted smile. Yet to self-enquire and to hover over the edge of the abyss of loss is literally terrifying for them. They want more, new and different rather than safe, honest and secure. They often talk fast, play hard and are gone before they get up chasing the next 'escape' route. They are escaping from themselves and an existential crisis that is a desolate annihilation.

Money Meditation: There is safety and richness beyond any of my wildest dreams inside the unknowable blueprint of my life. But to receive the gifts of the blueprint I must commit to at least a few dedicated tasks or career choices. It will be tough working through the salt mine of desolation, but I trust it will be worth it. If I do, Heaven and Earth will be mine.

Money Wound Antidote: I commit to being myself; to truly getting to know myself. The question, *'Who is the person behind the ever-changing facade?'* is a worthy and lifelong endeavour. I will look at my finances in a fresh way that is built in reality, sobriety and a future. I don't need a hundred back-up plans. I need just one or two solid and grounded plans to start with. I replace my old mantra of *more, new and different* with *enough, familiar and constant.* When I am grounded and have taken care of myself there will be plenty of time for spontaneity and adventure. I will finally get to enjoy my pursuits as I will be more present and filled with a calm invitation into the future that springboards from the Now.

Type Eight

If I am powerful or wilful, I will receive money
(Love/Trust/Security)

Attachment Style: The source of care was either physically or emotionally abusive, with times of excessive humiliation, exploitation and punishment. Or they had to 'survive' in some way, for example as rocky start to life such as premature or illness. As such the infant set the automatic pilot to 'fight mode' as a strategy to have their biological needs met.

World View: *'I need to remain tough and to protect myself to get ahead financially.'* This is the personality structure Type Eights bring to their money world view. The underlining belief system for Type Eight is, *If I had been stronger and more assertive, I could have protected myself in my formative years.'* This is sadly absurd. The Type Eight takes on a *'Never again'*, *'At all cost'* attitude when dealing with money. A very succinct illustration of Type Eight at work financially is the ruthlessness that can emanate from the boardroom. Type Eight has a caustic sense of loss of 'essential truth'. Type Eight fail to see that strength and power can take many forms. A cyclone can fell a huge tree while a blade of grass yields and survives the cyclone's wrath. They can become demanding bullies oblivious to the consequence of their words and deeds. The Type Eight can throw a grenade, turn around 360 degrees and sincerely ask, *'What happened? Why is everyone dead on the floor?'*

When Type Eights are under financial stress or pressure their wound of threat, humiliation and fear of punishment shows up. They are reminded how their 'first need' or 'essential impulse' to literally call or cry out to get their needs met and to feel safe was ignored, rebuffed or aggressively shut-down. In severe cases Type Eights were punished or abused. To survive they grew a thick skin, toughened up and became the boss of their own survival.

Money Mask: The corporate world is literally awash with Type Eights. To deflect at all cost, any possibility of feeling that excruciating primary impulse, they seek to conquer their world with control, wilfulness, dominance and non-emotionality. The kind of non-emotionality that puts profits before people, exploitation before nature. Their compensatory style can either be terrifying and/or charismatic. They use intimidation and fear without any thought for consequences. Most Type Eights see themselves as doing the job that needs to be done without obfuscating the take with redundant and emotional questioning. Type Eights expect collateral damage and sacrifice from others and are personally unwilling to adhere to the same set of principles.

Sympathetically, Eights fear vulnerability and weakness because it is a gateway to excruciating memories of their first and most significant core wound opening up. Unfortunately Type Eights feel alone, ostracised and isolated. They bolster themselves against other people and life. It can literally be very lonely at the top.

Money Meditation: The meditation for Type Eight is a simple recognition that conquering, even The World, will never be enough. If you wish to conquer any world then conquer the world within. This takes the strength of the giant oak and the humility of the blade of grass. Rather than feel their pain Type Eights will assert their will and bend the will of others. Financially they can be the poorest richest people in the world.

Money Wound Antidote: I will practise the art of listening. I will learn impulse control. I will feel the blades of grass beneath my feet and I will reflect under the shade of a magnificent tall tree. The power of nature, silent, humming or deafening, will speak to me of true strength. I will contemplate the consequences of my words and deeds. I will ask for honest reflection from family, friends and colleagues when I feel I am resilient enough from within. Protection from life is an illusion. A defensive life is a lonely and exhausting existence. I surrender to life's will and I ask that I am able to cultivate *'the serenity to accept the things I cannot change, the courage to change the things I can, and the wisdom to know the difference.'*
~ Reinhold Niebuhr

Type Nine

If I merge, I will receive money
(Love/Trust/Security)

Attachment Style: The source of care was miserly. The Type Nine did not experience unconditional love and faithful attention, either physically or emotionally. The biological needs were offered with an extreme lack of fundamental care and tenderness. The care is received as an indifference to whether the infant thrived or even survived.

World View: *'The world has forgotten me, so I will forget myself — I am forgettable. I am not worthy of being seen.'* This is the painful belief which forms the structure of the Type Nine. They did not receive that 'essential love' for their existence. With this self-forgetting, the Type Nine expands into a state of unworthiness and an extreme negation of self-value. This permeates through their financial world. They surrender their needs in order to assist other people's needs. They are over-looked for promotion in their chosen careers. They become the invisible backbones of a company that fails to see them. They wholeheartedly merge with the other to feel any self-worth or purpose.

Their lack of un-remarkableness to themselves can be reflected in their lifestyles, bank balances and even their business ventures. If you have ever seen two cafes side-by-side with one booming and the other failing, you could assume that a Type Nine is running the failing cafe into the ground.

Having no or little internal compass for their own meaningfulness or worthiness, Type Nines can feel burdened with the task of looking after themselves financially. They can have very low incomes, long periods of unemployment, neglect their money management and constantly fail to pay their bills on time. They are the people on the merry-go-round who continually move from one hobby-horse to the next, looking to merge and find a sense of purpose with the new hobby-horse and failing to see they are eternally going around in circles.

Type Nines have a meekness with money. This is reflected in low financial aspirations, an acceptance of living on very little and often living on the poverty line. To survive, they too hitch their wagons to others, not as a high ideal, but rather as a mechanism for their own survival. At their worst Type Nines merge and blur boundaries with others, becoming like a supplicating dog at the table waiting for crumbs.

Money Mask: As merging is less desolate than their internal landscape, Type Nines use the merging with other people's financial successes as a way of narcotising. They often look vague. They start many tasks and finish very few. They can be diplomatic and placating which hides the rage of their core wound. They hate being invisible and they hate standing out alone. They merge for survival.

Money Meditation: You have a right to be here. Your very birth is testament to that. Your breath in this moment is confirmation of your right to be here and to belong. You are precious and whole – seen or unseen. The universe in all its great expanse will miss an integral piece, a thread in the fabric of itself, when you are gone. In the meanwhile, your presence here amongst us is valuable. Know that, bring it into your heart.

Money Wound Antidote: I am here. I belong here. I value my autonomous, individual contribution to the whole. Both big and small. I have a right to say YES. I have a right to say No. I have a right to say, *'Can I think about that and get back to you.'* I am curious and energised by my journey of self-discovery: to know myself as separate from other people and fully connected and engaged with My Life. My Life includes other people. My sense of self comes from within. I look forward to choosing when and how I merge with other people. I am unique and valuable. There is no one quite like me.

Chapter 8

EXPOSING THE MONEY WOUND

"And the day came when the risk to remain tight in a bud was more painful than the risk it took to blossom." ~ Anaïs Nin

One of the most important aspects I want you to glean from *The Billionaire Buddha* is this: when it comes to *money wounds*, we are all in the same leaky lifeboat. Doesn't matter if we got in that boat from the 5-star luxury first class cabin or we were the stowaway. We can all improve our lives by respecting ourselves enough to respect our relationship with money. I have my wounds and you have yours. Anyone who truly believes they have no issues around money is denying themselves a fantastic journey of discovery. Working collaboratively will help our lifeboat from sinking: while a few keep the leak at bay by removing the incoming water, others can keep an eye out for ships, others can catch fish while others prepare food. When the hundred monkeys collaborate, miracles can happen. So here I put myself forward as one of the monkeys, one of the people sitting in that leaky lifeboat.

A couple of years ago I attended a course called *The Millionaire Mind Intensive*, by T Harv Eker. A fabulous three-day event I thoroughly recommend. A few of the processes in the course look at our upbringing around money. After finishing one such process which we did in small groups, all the participants came back together to share some of their insights to the greater group.

I put my hand up to share and to my terror, was chosen. I shared my history of stealing money. Even now I am quite surprised that I shared this information quite openly with around a hundred people. When I sat down, I was shaking, obviously the side-effect of deep exposure. A friend next to me commented, *'Gosh you are brave, I can't believe you just shared that with everyone.'* Not long after my share we went to a break and around forty people came up to me and expressed their gratitude of my courage of sharing something that had obviously caused me a lot of shame and how it had given them the courage to really look at some of the shame they have with their interactions with money.

I am not saying that you have to stand up in front of hundreds and share your wounds around money. But this, as well as many other moments in my 'recovery' of sorts, has shifted my psyche and definitely my heart around my relationship with money. The moment after my share I realised I wasn't alone.

When we are able to look frankly, truthfully, almost

brutally at our relationship with money and lay it bear for our self or others to see we can gain insights into our condition and the human condition around money. I am a great believer that money can make us noble or it can make us woeful with every nuance in between.

In my own personal and spiritual development, I use looking at the darker aspects of self as a quicker even more efficient way to the path of liberation. This is profoundly expressed here by the great Sufi mystic, Rumi.

"The cure for pain is in the pain"

If the thought of talking about something shameful to anyone is terrifying and fills you with dread, simply don't do it.

If the thought of talking about something shameful to anyone feels even the tiniest bit liberating, simply choose your confident carefully.

If you are undecided, simply do nothing.

If you want to talk to someone about possibly exposing some of your shame and past behaviours with money, to perhaps unburden yourself, simply find a kind therapist you like and with whom you could build trust and rapport or come and work with me.

At all costs … be kind to yourself and be measured with your decision.

By the end of this book your feeling around all this may change. Your need to speak or your need for silence could disappear with your shame!

Chapter 9

THE MONEY MASK

"A kind of mask, designed on the one hand to make a definite impression upon others, and on the other to conceal the true nature of the individual."
~ Carl Jung *"*

As we enquire into the *money wounds,* we get to see the 'Money Mask'. All the ways we hide the truth about what is actually going on in our relationship with money.

Carl Jung spoke of our mask as our *persona* or the *conformity* cloak that helps us to fit in with family, friends, peers, etc.

It's the outward face that we show the world. Whilst our *true* face stays hidden; our worries, stress, sense of entitlement, jealousy, anger, envy etc., all operate under the mask.

The *money mask* is our defence mechanism that stops us from truthfully looking at or expressing our accurate relationship or situation with money. We prefer denial and delusion over the exposure of our true money face. It works so unconsciously and automatically that we may not even notice it. The *money mask* is all the parts of our self in relation to money that we wish to cover up, not acknowledge, find unacceptable, because of an inherited belief system or a firm mental construct.

For example, the *money mask* may slant a story around money where we may feel justified or righteous. Or how we may cover the truth about our financial situation. It may stop us from really acknowledging our error in a particular money interaction. Or it can make us behave ruthlessly, greedily and indignantly. The *money mask* shows up when we want to disown, or it's too painful to acknowledge, a particular aspect of our *money wound*.

One of the biggest insights around my own *money mask* happened about ten years ago. I was in the habit of wearing a lot of gold jewellery and tried to dress to give the impression that I had a lot of money even though my bank balance knew I was lying. I often put on an air that I didn't really need to work and didn't correct people when they made that assumption about me.

The truth was I still had to work for the lifestyle I had chosen. I wasn't completely financially independent. When I looked at this mask, I realised the source came from the belief that I should have been more successful and financially freer by the age of forty. Obviously, this arbitrary time goal was embedded within my psyche — I still can't recall a specific moment when I took that belief on. Nevertheless, it was there. This wound caused me no end of pain and the mask, must have looked ridiculous.

By that I mean it wasn't fool proof — it bordered on cliché. I was getting no closer to financial freedom trying to sustain a wardrobe and jewellery box I couldn't afford. Ten years on the wound is still here but only a faint apparition that appears occasionally to keep me in check. As for the mask for this wound? After some digging and squirming and self-enquiry, I have dropped it.

We are conditioned to distance ourselves from our true motivations and true selves. We put on masks we believe will be more acceptable to the world than the truth of who we are. In doing so we sacrifice the gift of self-acceptance. The mask is used so we don't expose those hidden aspects of ourselves that we disown or dislike. We have a fear that if we acknowledge, or if others know the truth, we will be disliked and rejected. We have a terrifying fear that if exposed, love and respect, from external sources, will disappear.

Instead we reject our truth, our vulnerable precious truth, not realising that there are thousands, if not millions of people who also have the same reality as our own. Everyone, I repeat e-v-e-r-y-o-n-e, is too afraid to be the first to reveal their true and all but human identity. What we don't dare realise is that in rejecting this (our true selves) it causes us to suffer far greater and for far longer than if we were to just rip the Band-Aid (mask) off. Who wants to be a member of a club full of fraudsters? Paradoxically, it is when we own the shadow aspects of our self and put down the masks, we become truly loveable.

"Your heart is crying and weeping but you keep smiling. You try to hold on to your image. You cannot be natural, you cannot allow your heart, your body, your mind to function in a natural way. You keep manipulating them. You choose what can be expressed and what must be repressed." ~ Osho

Chapter 10

MONEY MASK ARCHETYPES

**"I am convinced that the deepest desire within each
of us is to be liberated from the controlling
influences of our own psychic madness or patterns of
fear. All other things — the disdain of ordinary life,
the need to control others rather than be controlled,
the craving for material goods as a means of security
and protection against the winds of chaos — are
external props that serve as substitutes for the real
battle, which is the one waged within the individual
soul."** ~ Caroline Myss

ۮ.١

The following *Money Mask* archetypes are a selected
illustration of the many masks we wear and show the world
as part of our relationship with money. Perhaps some of
them fit? Or perhaps you are starting to see a variation of
a mask that is mentioned here? Remember your *money
wounds* and masks are entirely unique. Keep exploring and

seeking clarity around healing these wounds. There are often many layers, and some are easy to identify, and some are a little more slippery.

The masks can show up as habitual behaviours, thoughts and belief systems that cover our *money wounds* and cloud our world view. We can more easily identify what mask may be operating in our life when we are experiencing pain and dysfunction around money. The circumstance and particulars of our financial suffering are reflected in the mind-talk (self-talk) we hear in our head or in the reoccurring difficult situations in which we may find ourselves.

We may have a *Money Mask* that is part of our personality structure: being fully identified with one's state of wealth (sense of power or importance) or poverty (sense of victimhood or collapse). We may switch *Money Masks* in certain circumstances to engender or manipulate certain outcomes. And some new or uncharted experiences might bring out the worst in us; a relative dies, and we turn into a complete money hungry bully fighting tooth and nail, burning all of our family bridges, for an inheritance we believe should be ours. A *Money Mask* can have both positive and negative presentations. They can support us or totally destroy us.

The work of identifying our *Money Masks* can be a liberating process whereby we see how we are ruled by our masks and kept in suffering. Negatively identifying with our *Money Masks* make us forget the amazing resilience, capability and strength we have as our birth right and which is accessible within the collective pool of human potential. We do ourselves a great physical and spiritual disservice by cowardly allowing the mask to speak for us. It's as if we give cart-blanche for an imposter to govern our lives.

Take a deep breath, all will be well. Remember you have the *28 Day Challenge* to put your money woes into recovery. If you are feeling overwhelmed — keep going! If you are feeling underwhelmed — keep going! If you are feeling really excited — keep going.

~

The Money Addict: The most obvious traits of the Money Addict are features like rife consumerism, retail therapy or over working in a bid to accumulate more, stealing or coveting other's wealth. The Money Addict has lost a lot of self-control and mindfulness of their behaviour for and around money. Guilt and shame can frequent the Money Addict when their addiction to consuming or possessing overrules their normal ability to be self-sustaining. The Money Addict is compensating for some deeper sense of lack, which usually has its source in feeling powerless or of low self-esteem.

The Poor Suffering Money Artist: There is a long list of individuals that have had this archetype rule much of their life, Van Gogh being one of the most famous. Essentially the Poor Suffering Money Artist has become so identified with the belief that money or reward for their unique contribution to the world does not come to them. This can often be projected as the *'world does not see my unique value.'* This archetype is very linked to self-esteem and a sense of self-worth. In contrast the artist can also rebel against the marketplace or financial system by rejecting money to their detriment as a form of self-preservation *'the world doesn't see how valuable I am, fuck'em.'* This archetype has lost faith in their individual unique value to the world and is strongly linked to the part in all of us that says, *'the artist in me will never survive, I better do something safe and predictable.'*

The Money Beggar: Seeing someone begging on the street in any major city around the world reminds us of this archetype's mask at play. So crippling can the Money Beggar archetype be, it can go on for generations and greatly increase behavioural problems, poor health and educational disadvantage for the children that they rear. The Money Beggar is not exclusive to those living on the street. We can all have a little of this archetype playing out in our life in some way and it calls us to confront self-responsibility in relation to money. Here the Money Beggar archetype speaks to us when we are disempowered in some way in relation to money, when we don't stand up for ourselves asking for more instead accepting the crumbs we might be given. The Money Beggar in us, is stuck in situations with money where we lack the power to choose and have personal authority. This could be in the lack of money, over-burdened with debt, whereby we do not have the choices money can bring.

The Money Bully: One of the most archetypal Money Bullies we see today is personified by entrepreneur and now President, Donald Trump. Many a biography and news article have told of Trump's business dealings being marred by aggression, exploitation and the occasional persecution of ordinary citizens opposed to his sprawling empire. The Money Bully in individuals uses money as a tool to bend the universe to their will. As a compensation to mask their deep sense of cowardice, intrinsic value and their *money wounds*, the Money Bully uses wealth, money and finances as a weapon to control their environment. A Money Bully dynamic can play out in personal or business relationships by withholding money, screwing someone down on price and blackmail. The act of sex trafficking and slavery are forms of The Money Bully at its absolute worst.

The Money Damsel & Money Knight Dynamic: Probably one of the most well-known representations of this dynamic is the Sugar Baby and the Sugar Daddy relationship. For the Money Damsel there is a lack of personal responsibility for their own survival. Where they wish or demand for their survival to be managed by another. The quality of the Money Damsel is reflected when we look to either an individual or external circumstance to be our financial rescue, rather than acting ourselves for our own survival. As for the Money Knight there is a certain sense of potency that is derived from being the provider. Of being wanted or needed, that their presence, albeit financial, is important or vital to someone else.

The Money Feminist: This archetype has arisen more in recent times with the advent of women taking on more financial independence. Beyond the concept that a woman is financially self-sufficient, identifying with this archetype can have a staunchness to it, *'I don't need anyone to support me financially, especially a man!'*

Of course, there are a lot of positives in this attitude of solitary self-reliance, but where the Money Feminist comes unstuck is in those moments of asking for help from others. Often this archetype has built this structure as a defence mechanism for not having anyone there for them financially, or they felt they could not rely on anyone, so they have built themselves a self-reliant mask, a form of protection against being let down financially.

Money Prostitute: Renowned speaker and bestselling author Caroline Myss' description of the Prostitute archetype best sums up The Money Prostitute for our purposes.

"The Prostitute archetype engages lessons in integrity and the sale or negotiation of one's integrity or spirit due to fears of physical and financial survival or for financial gain. This archetype activates the aspects of the unconscious that are related to seduction and control, whereby you are as capable of buying a controlling interest in another person as you are in selling your own power. Prostitution should also be understood as the selling of your talents, ideas, and any other expression of the self–or the selling-out of them. This archetype is universal, and its core learning relates to the need to birth and refine self-esteem and self-respect."
~ Caroline Myss

The Money Prostitute calls us to look at our self in relation to survival. How we may sacrifice our integrity or values in order to keep ourselves fed, clothed or sheltered. Aspects of the Money Prostitute operating in our life could be in our work or relationships, whereby we may prostitute ourselves in working in jobs we hate or staying in loveless relationships because it gives us financial security. The positive aspect of this archetype is that it inspires us to connect with what is in our hearts, our values and our integrity. Used with awareness, we can learn where we may be falling short.

The Money Seducer/Seductress: The aspect of our structure or personality that is lured into the belief that life will be better with more money. It sets up the grass is always greener syndrome, that can have us eternally yearning and pining for more and more money. It is the impulse that drives us to buy a lottery ticket as a strategy to improve one's life. It is often played out in a repetitive mindset of, '*I am not, or my situation is not good enough*', thus I need to seek more and having more money will be the tool to change this. The Money Seductress in us is born from an inability to accept the self at a deeper level and accept the present moment, accepting fully where we may find our self; not arguing with what is. At its core there is a sense of self-hatred and un-comfortability in accepting what is, and the distrust in the unpredictability and unfoldment of life. So, the internal Money Seductress convinces us that seeking is the key to avoiding the discomfort.

~

These are just a few archetypes to help you understand how you operate with money. There are many more archetypes and often composite archetypes, for example, the beggar and the victim archetype merge frequently. There are so many combinations that a 'diagnosis' of one or two archetypes isn't possible or useful. It's a journey of deep self-enquiry and self-evaluation. As you learn more about yourself in the *28 Day Challenge* you will be able to explore more about the concept of archetypes. You can get creative describing your behaviour in archetypal form. It's often a great technique that therapists use to give a little distance from the pain and consequent behaviour that this ego-identification causes.

By that I mean you can talk about yourself as an archetype in the third person until you feel resilient and resourced enough to really own and take responsibility for the 'archetype's' behaviour and speak in the first person, *I*.

د.ا

Chapter 11

EXPOSING THE MONEY MASK

*"The most important kind of freedom is to be what
you really are. You trade in your reality for a role.
You give up your ability to feel, and in exchange, put
on a mask."* ~ Jim Morrison

₪

Exposing the Money Mask Enquiry

Let's look at the masks we adopt as a deflection
strategy so that we can shed some light on our complex
issues with money and money image-management.

- Looking back at the list of money mask archetypes,
  which mask/s resonated with you and why?
- Consider the archetypes that you really disliked and be
  open to the possibility that this money mask may be
  operating in your life in some way. Explore this in your
  journal.

- Write down all the ways this mask/s are played out in your life? For example, *'I am a Money Mask Prostitute when I feel incapable of leaving the job I hate.'*
- Take a moment to write about a specific situation or event when this mask/s was at its most apparent.
- What do you believe was the underlining shadow or disowned aspect of yourself that this/these mask/s was/were covering?
- Do you know the source of the original wound (a sharp memory might come to mind)? If not, what is your general feeling as to how and why this wound was formed?
- What situations trigger this wound? For example, *'With this particular group of peers, I always give the impression that I do not have to work'*.
- How could you bring more self-acceptance to this wounded aspect of yourself?
- What's behind the mask? In an imaginary world, where you are safe, take the mask off and speak your truth. What would you really like to say?

Chapter 9

THE BUDDHA & MONEY

"Money is like water, try to grab it and it flows away, open your hands and it will move towards you."
~ Buddha

Should you be inclined, the Buddha has many interesting things to say about money and wealth. The ancient sacred scripts in the Tipitaka give great wisdom. Most of which can be still applied today.

Here are a few contemplations …

' … *do not engage in these five types of business: business in weapons, business in living beings, business in meat, business in intoxicants and business in poison. These are the five types of business that a lay follower should not engage in.'*

~

'*Cultivate the wish to be wealthy by lawful means.*'

~

'*Strive for perfection of faith, perfection of virtue, perfection of generosity, and perfection of wisdom.*'

~

'*How to spend wealth? If a person; through faith, virtue, generosity, and wisdom; has obtained wealth, good reputation, long life, and a path to a good rebirth, then he uses his money to accomplish four good deeds. He makes himself, his family, as well as his friends happy; he avoids accidents; he supports genuine ascetics and priests.*'

~

'*Five benefits of getting rich: If a person is getting rich, he should get five benefits.*

A man who gets rich by hard work and lawful way, makes himself happy and glad. He can also make his parents, his wife, children, and his servants happy, glad by his wealth. He can make his friends and companions happy, glad. Ill luck is warded off, and he keeps his goods in safety. He makes the five offerings to kin, guests, spirit, kings and deities.'

~

'*Four kinds of happiness due to wealth: If a man has acquired wealth by energetic striving, by his strength, won by sweat, and lawfully gotten, there are these four kinds of happiness to be won by the householder: the happiness of ownership, the happiness of wealth, the happiness of debtlessness, the happiness of blamelessness.*'

~

'There are four qualities that lead to a person's happiness and well-being in this life: being perfect in initiative, being perfect in watchfulness, admirable in friendship, and maintaining one's livelihood in growth and harmony.'

~

'Four ways a family can hold onto its great wealth for long: look for things that are lost; repair things that are old or broken, be moderate in consuming food and drink, place a virtuous, principled woman or man in the position of authority.'

~

'The clever, wise one will use the wealth for himself and also help his relatives. In doing so, he will not be dispraised and will have a pleasant future.'

The Billionaire Buddha 28 Day Challenge

THE BLINDFUL TRUTH

INTRODUCTION

*"If you do not change direction, you may end up
where you are heading."* ~ *Lao Tzu*

6ι

When we know better, we do better.

The *28 Day Challenge* is to help you explore the self-
awareness tools that you can use to empower yourself to
do better in all areas of your life. And of course, giving
special emphasis on your financial security, abundance and
generosity. You will move from **Blindful**, to **Mindful** to
Kindful.

Firstly, we look at all those hidden beliefs and
patterns that lurk in the shadows (**blindful**), all the
sabotaging mechanisms that operate in our blindspots.
Secondly, we will cultivate awareness around our limiting

behaviours and coax (or sometimes drag) them from the shadows (**mindful**). Thirdly, as we flourish in life and with our finances, we learn to be **Kindful** ... to move into the realms of generosity, grace and flow.

Before you know it, all three aspects will be in divine harmony and operating simultaneously. This is when life gets exciting, satisfying and true success can emerge. Despite what you have been taught, true success is heralded in with angelic sighs and whispers. It is not fanfares, trumpets and roaring applause: it is quiet, peaceful and serene.

I promise that if you follow these guidelines in the *28 Day Challenge* your finances will improve. However, if you fully engage, the wisdom in your wallet will creatively find the right questions tailored specifically for you, and you will thrive in ALL areas of your life. You need to be always asking the questions that facilitate positive growth or an evolution in how you do life — and how you do money. This honest practice of self-enquiry is the cornerstone to any type of life-changing work and long-lasting results.

You can draw a line in the sand to past mistakes, but you can't just step over it and expect all your life and money troubles to disappear with that one step. Yes, it's an epic start, the essential first step. However, it takes time, energy and commitment to make lasting change. You must draw that line in the sand and commit to the journey of self-discovery in a kind and compassionate way that supports your future: healthier, wealthier and happier you! It is said that it takes 28 days to break a habit and for a new one to neurologically stabilise in the mind and brain.

Be ruthless with your commitment and gentle with your process.

I love the following poem. It is entirely sympathetic and accurate. I use it for myself and offer it to my clients. Read it every day and see where you are at. Use it as a barometer for your goals and aspirations in life. Contemplation and reflection are needed here. Let this poem be the mantra for your life and financial journeys of discovery.

~

AUTOBIOGRAPHY IN FIVE CHAPTERS by Portia Nelson

ONE

I walk down the street
There is a deep hole in the sidewalk
I fall in
I am lost ... I am hopeless
It isn't my fault
It takes forever to find a way out

TWO

I walk down the same street
There is a deep hole in the sidewalk
I pretend I don't see it
I fall in again
I can't believe I'm in the same place

But it isn't my fault
It still takes a long time to get out

THREE

I walk down the same street
There is a deep hole in the sidewalk
I see it is there
I still fall in ... it's a habit
My eyes are open
I know where I am
It is my fault
I get out immediately

FOUR

I walk down the same street
There is a deep hole in the sidewalk
I walk around it

FIVE

I walk down another street

~

In order to heal and grow stronger in your financial awareness you will need to look at all your blindspots about money. This is not so easy, they are called blindspots for a reason. Other people can often see them more readily than we can. So here you are going to dig deep with self-enquiry and also, if it feels safe, you can ask for reflection from those who love you and have your best interests at heart.

Interspersed between the theory will be exercises to enable you to leave the **Blindful** and move into the **Mindful** with regards to your actual finances, budgets, forecasts, etc. In effect, you will be taking stock, an inventory of where you are great with money, adequate with money and where you greatly need to improve with money.

Shedding a light on all your finances in your material landscape whilst examining and healing your psychological and emotional landscapes around money is the only way forward.

The only way out is in … Let's dive in.

P.S. Although we will go through the *28 Day Challenge* in chronological order, you may wish to repeat, revisit or spend more time with each section. Keep your commitment burning and yet go at your own pace that supports you in the context of your life responsibilities and commitments. Most days should take about 20-30 minutes of contemplation and journal work. Find a safe place to work without distractions. If you can't find that at home you could do it in the park, in the library, at a local church, even in your car. Treat yourself to a notebook or journal. It doesn't have to be fancy or expensive. I prefer working with lined sheets as it keeps my messy handwriting in check. If you are going to type and work digitally then make a special folder and back up your work.

Day One

What is all that mud and how did it get there?

Imagine a glass of muddy water; brown, swirling and uninviting. Let's say that's your life. What we want to do is distil the water so that it becomes crystal clear and nourishing. How do we do that? We simply remove the crap. Most of us can survive by not stirring the water and all the sediment and crap sink to the bottom. We can ignore it and yet all along we know it's still there and we'd flourish much more without it. The distillation process can be fun and sometimes a little confronting. It can bring up some shame and other unpleasant feelings. That's what we want ... Bring it on!

And yet please remember that at different stages and ages in our lives our resilience to face our **Blindful** truths waver. If you feel you need more support, then engage a therapist or do this challenge with a friend. Asking just one person for help expedites the process tenfold.

We are going to start by stirring the muddy waters even more by way of self-enquiry questions. In doing this we will simultaneously have greater clarity with our inventory.

Even though it might be a little confronting; lean into ruthless honesty. Just the facts. No interpretation or exaggeration needed. And practise positive framing when you write in your journal. Positive framing of your truths can change your fear-programs at far greater speed than negative ones. You might need to listen to the negative self-talk to get a spontaneous and honest picture about yourself and the belief system. But then re-frame it when you write it in your journal.

Q. How are you at saving money?

A. Negatively framed with exaggeration and interpretation.

'I am so crap. I am the worst. I can't save to save my life. Mum always said I was selfish, and I'd amount to nothing. What's the point … I am useless. I don't even earn enough to save anyway. I would if I could.'

A. Positively framed staying with just the facts.

'I have not had much success with saving so far and I'm determined to break this cycle. I can see myself with a lot of savings that will bring me security.'

Be honest and also bring into your awareness the visualisation of where you want to be. Never hold yourself to who you used to be. This is the great stumbling block for most people. A static false identification with a behaviour or pattern that can be altered with commitment. Believe in yourself. And if you don't believe in yourself, then you have 28 challenge days to prove yourself wrong.

Trust this process and *tether your financial camels*. In short, take responsibility with day to day money tasks. Pay your bills on or before their due date. Buy necessities always before any luxuries. Look at your budget every day or week (whatever works best for you). Have a rainy day lump sum. Look at superannuation and insurance ...

Argggghhhh — STOP! Here's the overwhelm.

Breathe. Yes Breathe. Help is here. You are not alone. We will explore strategies in how to get on-top of all of this. Breathe. Yes Breathe. Help is here.

1. Take a Financial Selfie

I want you to write down everything that's in your head about your finances. Don't look up things or try and be super accurate. Just make a bullet point list of the good, the bad and the ugly. If you forget anything ... well, there's a glaring blindspot. We want a brainstorm splurge not a reconciled spreadsheet. Here are some headers to get you started:

Liquid Assets
• Liquid assets (cash, savings, super, term deposits)

- Possible liquid asset (cash owed to you)
- Cash gifts you may get from family etc.

Hard Assets
- House
- Investment properties
- Car's depreciating value
- Computers / iPhone / iPad / Expensive Electronics
- Artwork
- Anything else you could sell if you had to and convert it into liquid cash.

Debts
- Debts to friends or family
- Debts to banks or finance companies
- Debts to car loan company
- Debt to smartphone / data provider
- Debt to lay-by or interest free credit
- Mortgage interest
- What do you pay in taxes (estimate)?
- Other salary sacrifices like Super?
- Other …

Money Coming In
- Current income and predicted certain incomes
- What do you earn a year / month / week?
- Second job? Airbnb?

Money Black Holes
- Tax returns owed
- A few different Super funds
- Share that you don't track
- Family trusts
- Credit Card Debts

- Looming repairs — house, car, computer etc.
- Anything that will need upgrading
- Life insurance and health insurance
- My own Will.

As you are writing all this down really check in to how it makes you feel. What self-talk comes up — negative or positive? Take a deep breath. This is the first step to respecting your finances. When you respect your money … you are respecting yourself and your life!

Day Two

Contemplation / Meditation

Take a moment to sit in a quiet place. Think about where you are right now with money and notice how that feels in your body. You may feel a tightening in your chest or a foggy brain. You can't get this wrong. Just notice how you feel and where you feel it.

Now turn your attention to where you would like to be in the near future with regards to money and financial freedom. Let yourself have fun here ... really imagine an abundance of money and the liberation that brings in the feeling body. Again, just notice where you feel the sensations in your body. In your journal write as much as you can about what financial freedom, financial security or financial serenity would mean to you, particularly using language on how it will make you feel.

Tune in to the commitment you have around doing this course. Often our commitment to the small steps are pretty accurate indicators of how we take the big steps. How we do some things, is how we do all things. Have you given yourself enough uninterrupted time to do the *28 Day Challenge*?

Of course, you can include some fears about old patterns arising, but I want you to really focus on is not just getting through this but also having fun and feeling the transformational energy that arrives when you engage, take responsibility and commit.

Find a quote or poem or some other sort of inspiration that you can print out and use as a motivating anchor. Ask your partner, family and friends for help. Share with them what you are doing and ask them to check in on your engagement and progress.

If you feel like a little more support you can check out my on-line guided meditations … always great for inspiration, relaxation or motivation.

JaneMonicaJones.com/meditations

Write in your journal now. And come back to here when you are done.

Ready to dig a little deeper? Let us enquire where we may be holding pain in relation to money and survival. Write as much as you can using these questions as prompts.

1. Growing-up what were the predominant beliefs, statements, sentiments and values conveyed in your household about money?

2. Are you more like one parent than the other around money or completely different?

3. What are your greatest pains and fears about you and money?

4. What are the greatest pleasures when thinking about money?

5. What are your greatest fears about your ability to survive?

Capture all these insights in your journal.

~

"In virtually every spiritual tradition, suffering is seen as a doorway to awakening. In the West, this connection can be seen in the biblical story of Job, as well as the dark night of the soul in medieval mysticism. The transformative power of suffering finds perhaps its clearest expression in the Four Noble Truths espoused by the Buddha. Though suffering and trauma are not identical, the Buddha's insight into the nature of suffering can provide a powerful mirror for examining the effects of trauma in your life." ~ Peter A. Levine

Day Three

What are you looking at?

"We are all of us in the gutter. But some of us are looking at the stars!" ~ Oscar Wilde

Every day we are getting a little closer to financial clarity ... the spreadsheet facts and the emotional facts. Keep trusting in the process and lean into the theory. Let it work its magic on your psyche.

It is a misconception of the majority of people who struggle with money that financial awareness is really too hard to get a handle on. Just that belief there will stop you in your tracks. But everyone has to work with money, so I invite you to look through a positive lens gazing up at the stars. If you look down ... well mostly you feel down.

Answer the following questions ... really try and dig a little deeper each time you feel a response arise. Ask yourself, *'Is there something that I'm not seeing here?'*

1. What were some of the values regarding money you were brought up with? List some of the common statements you often heard from your parents, teachers, religious care givers.

2. What is your greatest money secret? How does it make you feel when contemplating this secret?

3. What are some of the behaviours you feel a little shameful about you and money?

4. What are the repetitive thoughts you have when you compare yourself with others and their money or success?

Close your eyes. Take a few deep breaths and then stand up and shake it off. Shake your hands and your feet. If you are in a place that prevents this ... then do it in your mind's eye.

Now a few more practical questions ...

- Who is your accountant?
- How often do you see your accountant?
- What is your tax bracket?
- What is your gross pay and net pay and where does the difference go?

- Do you know a good bookkeeper?
- Who do you trust with financial advice ... and are they financially secure?
- What's your credit rating?
- What's the credit limit on your credit card?
- Do you pay off your credit card monthly and on time so as not to pay interest?
- How much does your credit card cost per year - the annual fee?
- What are the perks of your credit card and do you really use them?
- What's the interest rate on your credit card?
- What's the cash advance on your credit card?
- What are your bank fees and ATM charges per year?
- Do you look at your credit card statement each month and verify that it's correct?
- Do you play lottery or any other game of chance?
- How much money do you save each month and what is the interest earned on that amount?
- Are you owed a tax rebate?
- Are you entitled to any tax credits / offsets either personally, family or business?
- Are you tracking your spending with a smartphone app?
- Do you have a financial retirement plan?
- Do you have a one year, five year and 10-year financial plan? Goals not dreams
- What are your five biggest expenses each month?
- What are your predictable fixed expenses and what are your variable expenses?
- Do you have a tight budget or a nebulous budget?
- Do you feel you have adequate financial awareness to steer your Money Boat into an abundant future?

Now take a very deep breath and check in with yourself ... are you looking up or down right now? Either/Or and cross-eyed are all okay too.

Every day we are moving more and more to financial clarity. The good news is that the tough work is at the beginning and it not only gets easier but if you expand your financial awareness you will also have more money to play with and a happier disposition.

If you are so inclined to read up and increase your financial knowledge then go ahead, be my guest. If this sort of information will drive you to distraction, I suggest you learn enough to be able to ask the right questions ... then find a financial advisor, financial counsellor, an accountant, a bookkeeper to talk with and ask those questions. They might just be the best investment you will ever make.

Task List - choose A or B

A) Get abreast of your financial landscape.
B) Pay someone to get abreast of your financial landscape.

And in my experience the most successful people choose A and B.

Now go and do something that feels good ... make contact with another human being, preferably face to face, and tell them about the progress you're making and its only day three.

Day Four

Between the Spreadsheets

If I told you that doing the *28 Day Challenge* would make you a better lover and also irresistible, I bet you'd be a lot more focused. Well, the good news is that being secure, not worrying about money, growing your funds and assets will make you a happier, more relaxed and self-assured person ... everyone knows that's super sexy. Let's get down and dirty between the spreadsheets.

Think of getting into crisp, fresh, white linen sheets ... there's a fragrance like spring and an invitation to a great night's sleep. It's the same for spreadsheets ... keep them clean and tidy and when you pull back the top sheet and it reconciles; you'll be out like a light and sleep like a baby.

We are ironing out our emotional wrinkles and we are reconciling our financial wrinkles too. The following Pythagoras equation still holds true ...

Healthy Financial Emotions and Beliefs + Clean, Changed Daily Spreadsheets = A Good Life's Sleep

Write in your journal how you are now feeling about money ... be really honest here. Remember you cannot get this wrong. You are simply gauging if there is any shift in your consciousness and belief systems. All we are doing at this stage is preparing the muddy water for distillation.

Have a look at these beliefs and concepts around money. Which ones resonate and is there a backstory?

Explore in your journal these common beliefs and add some of your own. Try and be specific. Can you recall your mother or father or caregiver reciting a recurring catchphrase?

- Money begets money
- To be rich you have to be ruthless and have no scruples
- Rich people are greedy
- There is a reason rich people are described as filthy rich
- If you want riches you have to dig ditches
- Money is the root of all evil
- A fool and his money are easily parted
- Money and me, are not good friends
- I have no luck around money
- I want just enough to survive — I won't sell out

- Thinking about money sends me shopping or out drinking
- Money is 1% inspiration and 99% luck
- Work is a four-letter word
- I've been a total flake with money and now it's too late
- Christian, good people are happier being poor
- I'll never have enough so what's the point
- I'm an artist and everyone knows we die poor
- I'm just not smart enough to handle money
- Spend now … you can't take it with you
- Marry in your money class
- If I won the lottery, I wouldn't change much
- If I won the lottery, I'd take care of all my friends and family first
- I play the lottery every week and I just know I am going to win
- It's rude to talk about money, religion and politics
- I feel guilty about needing more money when there are so many people in real need
- I hate how I earn money — but we are all prostitutes in one way or another
- It's impossible to save on what I earn
- It's easier for a camel to pass through the eye of a needle than it is for a rich man to enter the kingdom of Heaven
- I just need to have a good financial buffer in the bank before I can relax and even think about financial security
- Accountants and bookkeepers are so BORING
- I hope to marry rich
- I don't want to die poor.

If you truly analyse them … which ones are absolutely true, as in always true for everybody? Or can you see that these may be concepts and beliefs that might be limiting and/or untrue. There is no right or wrong, just awareness. Now have a go at reframing into the positive some of the statements that ring true for you. For example,

'I've been a total flake with money and now it's too late.' To *I haven't had my attention on money and recognise that I can change that at any age.'*

'I'm an artist and everyone knows we die poor.' To *'I'm an artist and some artists make it big … why not me?'*

Try uncovering these core beliefs either by journaling or exploring more with your therapist. Keep unpacking them and play with rewriting them into the positive. When you have a list of positive affirmations about money print them out and read them every day. And remember that affirmations and visualisations are powered by worldly actions and objective awareness.

Change and update your mind set and your spreadsheets regularly … this is one sure way to stimulate growth and realise potential.

"If you change the way you look at things, the things you look at change." ~ Wayne Dyer

Day Five

Get out of your own way

So here is where we get right up in the face of self-sabotage. The saboteur works in clandestine collusion with your covert beliefs. We have to recognise our symptoms (self-sabotaging behaviours) before we can cure them. This can be confronting, and a lot of shame and negative self-talk can accompany the simple facts. What I would like you to do is just focus on the simple facts.

Let's explore all the barriers within yourself that you have built against and around money. Do both exercise a) and b).

a) For the affirmation/manifesting and fixed mindset types ...

If you are the kind of person constantly listening to abundance meditations, reading manifesting and wealth creation self-help books, doing exercises to *'change your mindset'*, doing affirmations, building vision boards, spending a small fortune of money on self-help courses, chanting *'If I believe, I will receive'*, doing gratitude practices, seeking ways to feel profoundly worthy deep within your soul and any past souls you may have had, you will want to truly expose this.

If you were never allowed to do any of these practices again with regard to money and survival, what would happen to you, how would you feel and what would you think?

Imagine you without those external habits. What are you sensing in your body? What are you feeling? What thoughts are coming to mind? Write everything down. Let it flow uncensored: thoughts, feelings, words, resistance, sensations in the body, painful contemplations, fears etc. Be as specific as possible.

~

b) For the planner, strategising, analysing types …

If you continually analyse your financial positions, constantly checking stocks, drawing up profit projections, delving into superannuation projections, contemplating which financial strategy is the best strategy, feel you need to discover 'that' edge, try to analyse how friends, family or colleagues have become wealthy, looking for the next big idea, your need to examine why and what it gives you and denies you.

If you were never allowed to do any of these practices again with regard to money and survival, what would happen to you, how would you feel and what would you think?

Imagine you without those external habits. What are you sensing in your body? What are you feeling? What thoughts are coming to mind? Write everything down. Let it flow uncensored: thoughts, feelings, words, resistance, sensations in the body, painful contemplations, fears etc. Be as specific as possible.

~

When you have exhausted all you think is in there, look over all you have written. Everything listed here are your pain points or fear points around money. These are the weak points where your saboteur resides.

- What are the primary fears you have about you and money?
- How are these fears being played out in your life?
- What destructive behaviours do you have in relation to money?
- Where in your life have you not defended yourself in relation to money and others?
- What were the primary feelings and thoughts you have used as justification why you may not have defended yourself in the above situations?
- Have you let financial opportunities pass you by?

- Can you recognise the Saboteur operating in others' financial lives?
- What would be the advice you would offer them in managing their financial Saboteur?

"I decry the injustice of my wounds, only to look down and see that I am holding a smoking gun in one hand and a fistful of ammunition in the other." ~ Craig D. Lounsbrough

Day Six

Put your affairs in order ... you are about to live!

"Organising is something you do before you do something, so that when you do it, it is not all mixed up." ~ A.A. Milne

Today we are looking at the order and the chaos in our lives.

Simple ... look around and see what's shoved in drawers, under the bed, in the garage, out of sight and out of mind.

Time to come clean ... if you need help in organising, filing, decluttering, systemising etc. then get help! This is the second most important investment you can make in your new prosperous life. If you can't find anything then you can't sort it out.

You need to get a system of organisation that works for you. To get some ideas, have a google around and see what other people do. Go to Office Works, Office Depot (whatever it is called in your region) and ask the staff ... get creative. And above all ... KISS

Keep It Simple Silly!

- How do you file bills? Paper or Online?
- How do you know if you've paid a bill?
- Are you recording all incoming and outgoing money?
- Do you have a back-up of files and folders?
- Is your online banking user friendly?
- Do you have your bank's smartphone app?
- Do you have an app that tracks spending?
- Do you have a savings account setup?
- Do you use Excel or an accounting software?
- Do you keep all receipts and how are they filed?
- Are your tax returns up to date?
- Does your bookkeeper and accountant love your system?
- Can you put your hands on all your legal, insurance, financial, tax documents, mortgages, wills etc?
- In the event of your accidental death could your executer readily understand your filing and easily access all relevant documents to execute your will and close down your estate? (This one is an important one, don't leave your financial mess to your loved ones. You want them to have fond memories of you ... not annoying or frustrating ones!)

- Are warranties and guarantees filed in one place?
- Are your credit cards and ID backed up?
- Are your direct-debits and auto-payments in order?
- Do you have a file/document or app with all your myriad of digital account logins etc?

Of course, this is highlighting that a modern life is filled with papers and documents and all sorts of reporting and accounting systems. If you have an easy to follow daily or weekly rhythm of organisation it will save you so much time in the long run.

It might take a little while to get your systems in place … but make a start today. Tackle one thing at a time. You need to get a mental and physical map of how your money flows and where it goes.

Imagine … the easier this gets, the faster this gets, and you might just see a way to improve or start a business. Mapping your finances like this is the precursor to successful business.

Mind your own business, then mind your own businesses.

Day Seven

"You must gain control over your money or the lack of it will forever control you." ~ Dave Ramsey

A lot of spending is mindless habit, for example, food shopping without price or buying too much and wasting it can be a huge hole in your bucket. Buying expensive brands just for the label that's not even shown. Only you may know your black simple V-neck cotton T-shirt is a Lacroix, to most people it could be a Bonds T-shirt worth $3. It's not really about what we are spending our money on but rather the stories we tell ourselves to justify our purchases. If we are spending without a thought for consequences, then inevitably this will be reflected in how we are able to participate in life. Of course, it's all relative but the old adage still applies: 'Look after the pennies and the pounds will look after themselves.' (Read cents and dollars.)

We need to pay attention to how we use money ... or it can start to use us up.

Some of our spending can be unacknowledged self-harm. How much do we spend on alcohol, cigarettes, junk food, processed foods and as a result of making poor health choices? How much are we spending on medicines or vitamins and herbal supplements to fix all the careless **blindful** self-harm?

What I am pointing to here is the unconscious habits of spending. It's not about abstinence or excess, it's about more awareness of behaviours, re-evaluating old decisions and making more appropriate choices. The habit of spending can be a huge hole in your pocket. There is no wisdom in doing something that you chose to do when you were younger or yesterday; that didn't serve you then and doesn't serve you now.

Fine tune your spending awareness. We can agonise for days or weeks over a big purchase and yet inadvertently flit away thousands of dollars on ephemeral and instant gratification purchases. Be mindful of this sometimes habitual area of your life.

From today and at least until the end of this challenge I want you to track your spending. Again, there are plenty of good Apps for your smartphone. Most are free. You just need a basic tool. You could even use a small notebook and pen. For some of you this will be a relief, and quite enjoyable. And for some of you it will be tedious, and you might feel your rebel come to the surface kicking and screaming.

It's an exercise to gain a true reflection on your spending habits and motivation for spending. Keep a track of what goes on for you emotionally. Are there particular people or events that trigger your spending? Think about how this relates to the *money wounds* in this book. Journal and explore what arises, especially the shame areas around money. What is the narrative, the voice(s) in your head telling you?

This can be one of the most life-changing aspects in this course. A simple realisation about your relationship with money.

If you are already a money tracker and you'd still like to understand your relationship with money more, it might just be a question of asking the questions ... Did I really need this purchase? What do I believe it gave me? Was it lasting? What is the core wound trying to be filled, behind this? Does the critical judge come in, as you contemplate all of this? What does it say? Remember that this challenge is about not making sweeping changes right away. It's not about judging yourself. Like all self-enquiry you are being asked to put yourself under a microscope and just observe. As best as you can stay with the facts without interpretation. Like a scientist ... observe, take notes and let the process integrate within you. Be kind to yourself.

Enquiry Journaling Exercises

- How easy is it to embrace tracking all your spending?
- What are you excited or afraid to find out about yourself?

- What does your spending really say about you?
- Have a look at your emotional motivation for spending … are there nuances or blindspots here?
- What resistance arises and how does it manifest in you? Do you rebel, collapse, self-criticise or something else?
- Check in with your commitment here to finish this challenge … how firm is your commitment to keep going? No judgement. It might be good to notice how you may waiver around commitment.

Remember to be kind to yourself. Take notice of negative self-talk and strong judgements, they often turn up when we are seeking change in our life; it is very natural part of the exposure process but remember do not identify with what they are saying. If a judgement arises … remind that inner critic that you are committed to doing better with money and to back off!

Day Eight

"Rest is not idleness, and to lie sometimes on the grass under trees on a summer's day, listening to the murmur of the water, or watching the clouds float across the sky, is by no means a waste of time."
~ John Lubbock

This is the most important day so far. The day of rest and recapping. Have a glance through your journal with a sense of achievement. Some minds will step in here and say, *'I've done more than enough!'* Some minds will step in and say, *'You could have done so much more!'* Few minds will have the Goldilocks mentality and think they've done just enough.

What I am asking you to do here is override that inner critic and simply stay with the facts. You committed to starting a journey. You have started. You need to acknowledge what you have done. Go over it in some leisure time. Let it integrate in a gentle way. Trust that what you need to remember will come to your mind's eye when needed. It's time to relax.

It's time to go on a 'date', night or day, with yourself. It's about making time to take care of your rest cycles and your reward cycles. These are possibly the most important aspects to managing your money in a **kindful** way. What's the point of working yourself to exhaustion and then taking an all too infrequent holiday or having a 'relaxing' night out? For many people just to get into the zone of relaxation they might drink way too much or spend way too much. Feels relieving in the moment, but helps you take two steps back the next day ... or when the credit card bill arrives.

I'm suggesting 'date' time in nature, with good healthy food, nature-exercising, catching up with close friends, have a massage, treat your partner to a massage ... any kind of activity that involves being in the body and away from the busy doing mind. What about a classical concert? Anything that might soothe the nervous system rather than over stimulate it.

I really want you to get that the true measure of success is not how much money you have but how much leisure and self-care time you have ... and not only how much but also the quality. A measure of quality time is how present you were and how much you can savour and remember. This might be a good time to look at your relationship with self-care and rest. Life does not always have to be higher, faster, stronger. Sometimes it can be slower, gentler and deeper.

Practise this simple sensory awareness exercise to cultivate true grounded presence.

What can I smell right now? What can I see right now? What can I hear right now? What can I feel through my skin right now? (Hot cold, breeze, wet, dry) What can I taste right now?

Then practise a deeper awareness scan of your body.

What can you feel in your head, throat, heart, belly, base/sex, then end with feet? Just a two minute scan of noticing YOU in the body YOU inhabit. Who is witnessing and commenting on the sensory input? It's really worth contemplating as you deepen into this process of being more authentically you and examining what has shaped you over your entire life, but especially your formative years.

Snooze, sleep, power nap, do nothing, stare at a tree, plant flowers or veggies, lie in your garden or a park, play with your pet ... make a deeper connection with yourself and enjoy it.

You might even surprise yourself.

Day Nine

Gratitude and Positivity

"Acknowledging the good that you already have in your life is the foundation for all abundance."
~ Eckhart Toll

Feeling abundant and happy have been directly linked to the practise of Gratitude. You can't lose. If you're truly appreciative of what you have and find an inner peace with having enough, then having more becomes merely a bonus. Make what you have count and celebrate and share the bonuses.

Gratitude Process #1 ... for the rest of your life
• On waking think and write down three things you are

grateful for in your life
- On getting into bed think and write down three things you are grateful for in your life.

Don't keep writing the same things or the obvious things. Spread your gratitude net wide and far.

Positivity Process … for the rest of your life

Find a time in the day or evening that works for you and journal a positive experience that you have had. Perhaps it was a lucky win, a synchronistic meeting, you met your partner, your child was born, your puppy arrived … It's not important what it was but rather that you can capture, imagine and vividly recall this event.

It will help the neural pathways re-live the experience as an echo. The more and more we re-live these echoes the more and more the brain is being rewired to look for positive experience.

We are bombarded with negativity and bad news. It's relentless. There is an old expression that I use as a self-check tool:

"There are three types of business; your own business, everyone else's business and God's business. If you are in any other business than your own … then you're in trouble."

Of course, we cannot live in a vacuum and be entirely insular, yet we can monitor and cut down on the amount of negative input we have from the outside world; a world outside of our own control. It entrenches feelings of despair and powerlessness. Just switch off and move your attention to something positive in your sphere of influence. End the day on a happy note … and see how this permeates into your sleep and dreaming.

Gratitude Process #2 … for the rest of your life

At least once a week express your gratitude in a detailed way. By that I mean not just a quick emoji. Let someone know what they mean to you and why. Let them know that they are seen, heard and appreciated — it's all any of us ever really want. Just some small acknowledgement that we belong and that our presence and relationships have meaning and are important. It just needs one or two people to appreciate us and for us to have one or two people whom we appreciate to alleviate depression, loneliness and the existential disconnect that the 21st Century offers.

~

Rather than give you the statistics here about how these two practices really change your mindset and can ultimately change your life, I want you to just do the practice and see what happens. Don't just read about statistics; be the statistics. There is heaps of information about happiness on the internet and some great talks at Ted.com.

Day Ten

Focus on the Positives — Positivity Positively Supports Happiness!

"You can't make positive choices for the rest of your life without an environment that makes those choices easy, natural, and enjoyable."
~ Deepak Chopra

One of the most exciting things about living and learning in the 21st Century is the amount of empirical data research we have that supports historic spiritual or new age ideas. We know now that the brain re-wires itself and in turn has an 'echo' or 'shadow' effect on our DNA. Science tells us that being positive can have a dramatic effect on our ability to create and affect those around us. Even a forced smile changes the neural chemistry and can actually make you feel better. So, faking it until you make it isn't so bad at all.

We are going to now look at what is working in our financial life. Read this whole next section with a smile on your face. Do you notice anything at all? Do the following exercise with the biggest cheesiest grin on your face.

In your journal write down all the income streams you have. What money comes in and through what stream?

Look at all the money and income you have in your life. For most people this is going to be quite simple. Also write down gifts, someone shouts you a coffee, birthday money from relatives — any and all types of income. Perhaps you get paid for a home business, a service or a product. Perhaps you are paid in kind ... you swap massages, baby-sitting, driving etc. Look at all the 'positive' flows coming into your life, not just the warm soft cash.

If you are on salary ... get up close and personal with that. Understand what you are paid gross and net, what you are taxed, what tax bracket you are in, exactly what taxes are taken out, what other contributions come out of your pay, what levies are deducted etc.

Now I want you to think of all the times that you feel you were lucky with money, caught a break, won something in life, someone was kind to you, perhaps a random act of kindness from a stranger, an upgrade, found a dollar or two on the street, found a twenty dollar note in an old jacket or pair of jeans, the perfect gift someone gave you ... all the times you just felt lucky. Really spend a moment acknowledging the flow of money. This is not magic, it's just what money energy does. Money is a lot like water ... it always finds the path of least resistance.

Still got that face grinning?

That's what we are doing here ... stirring the glass of muddy water ... removing the silt and creating pathways for money to flow towards you and altruistically from you. Focus on your breath while simply accepting that this is how money as an energy works. There's no big *Secret* !!!

So now let's get down to some more accountability and let's at least go in here with a good feeling ... financially the more we know the more we grow.

Practical Exercise — Assets

These should get easier and easier the more you become familiar with your financial landscape. List all the liquid assets you have and also the hard assets. Any ready-cash available and also anything that would be deemed a luxury that you could sell. List the sellable items for their true current worth ... not what you paid for it and not what you hope to get for it. Go on the internet and do a price comparison. Be optimistic and realistic.

Warm Soft Cash

- Bank Balance (what is the interest rate and what are the bank fees?)
- Cash around the house and in your wallet

- Cash you could get access to quickly
- Investments (what are average dividends and fees?)
- Stock / Shares / Bonds (what are average dividends and fees?)
- Property (what is average income and fees?)

Sellable Items

- Car
- Bikes
- Electronics
- Computer
- Kitchen Appliances
- Furniture
- Spares of anything
- Art or jewellery

List anything to remind yourself of what you have acquired ... again anything that has come into your life. You may never sell any of these things but again when thinking positively we want to remind our brain and its neural pathways that we have achieved and do have relative success. This is about embodying the good feelings around our material gains and not focussing on the lack. Can you hear your mind chatter here? What are some of the things your mind is saying right now? Write them down. If they are negative ... please cross them out and reframe it in the positive. The aim is to have a true objective relationship to money and the things it buys. Some things are worthless financially and yet sentimentally mean the world to you. Examine all the ways in which you might be emotionally engaged with your things. Again, leave the judgement out of it. Just be honest. Financial clarity starts with emotionally honesty.

If you are self-employed, a sole-trader or freelancer then part of your responsibility is to know your cashflow inside and out. And if you cannot or simply don't want to then you must employ someone who does. Knowledge is power when it comes to money. Managing your own income and expenditure when taken seriously can facilitate a lot of freedom and fun. Tracking jobs, multiple income streams, cash and digital payments, all take on a very different gravitas as opposed to simply receiving a pay cheque each month. In short ... you must know about taxes (income and sales taxes) and you must siphon money for taxes in a preferably high interest savings account. Are you also paying into a superannuation fund for your retirement? So many of my clients have been freelance, great entrepreneurs and creatives yet due to lack of money management know-how they have ended up with very little to show for their hard work, inspirations and efforts.

~

- Journal what has come up for you in this chapter and what you are feeling around it all.
- Do you feel optimistic or has the negative self-talk plummeted you into a pessimistic cycle?
- Feeling richer or poorer?
- Grateful and realistic or something else?

Remember to always track the emotions in the body ... get a sense of where they appear in the body, for example, hot or cold, tight chest, constriction in throat, pain in the eyes ... track your body. Then stand up and shake it out.

Day Eleven

Recap!

"Wealth is the ability to fully experience life."
~ Henry David Thoreau

If we break this down philosophically, we are discovering that it's not how much money you have that makes you wealthy but the capacity, ability, and the bounce-back resilience to fully experience and engage in YOUR life that makes you a happy success.

It's time to go read your journal in sync with the past chapters. We have completed ten full days. It's been a journey of emotional self-enquiry and honesty and also objective clarity around finances.

At this stage you might not be feeling exceptionally clear about your relationship with money, but you should be feeling a glimmer of hope and also a sense of control as you empower yourself with knowledge.

You have explored:

1. Your financial Selfie (what was in your awareness)
2. The courage to contemplate your emotional landscape and money
3. Your truer financial picture with some hard hitting questions
4. Your belief systems around money
5. Some of your fears and self-sabotaging strategies around money
6. How to get organised and efficient with money
7. Bringing awareness to habitual spending and unconscious spending
8. Relaxation around this process and your relationship to life and money
9. Gratitude and positivity around money
10. Focusing on the positives whilst looking at the nitty-gritty and what needs changing.

Journaling Exercises

- Write down what you enjoyed the most
- Write down the key take-away lessons for you
- Write down what surprised you most
- Write down five ways in which you are going to improve with your money management
- Write down what shifts for the better are occurring as you gain awareness of your money relationship.
- What has been an insight or gift from this process?

Essential Budget Time

It's time to write out a new budget. One that is based in reality and necessities. In this particular budget you are not going to write down any entertainment, massages, new shoes, new car accessories, latest Mac, Samsung Galaxy, iPhone, make-up etc. Just write down, now that you have a clearer knowledge, everything that you need to keep your life going. Just the basics.

Make sure you account for everything including possible car repairs and items you know need attention or a service etc. Base this budget on your realistic spending habits. Don't tell yourself you can spend less on food without having tested it out. Be realistic, not harsh. Remember dental visits, private health insurance deductions, cloud storage or internet subscriptions etc. Weigh up what is essential and what is necessary. This will vary slightly for each individual.

If you can write this on a spreadsheet on your computer then all the better. Familiarising yourself with Excel or Numbers will save you a lot of time in the long run. And if you just want to do this in your journal for now that's okay too. When you have done your budget ask someone who knows you if they can ensure you haven't missed anything out. Remember we are moving from **Blindful** to **Mindful**. Be kind with yourself. It's a great exercise to do with a friend or partner. It's often amusing how we define or justify necessities.

Now simply write down what your net income is next to what your total essential budget expenditure is. What's the difference? How much do you have over for luxuries, entertainment, holidays and savings?

If there's not much left … then you need to think about earning more money or downsizing. Don't panic about either just yet. This is just part of the process. I'm simply asking you to be realistic about how much you might need to keep you safe, fed, in connection with friends and family and most importantly with an achievable proportionate sense of happiness

Day Twelve

Reconcile Your Past

"Too many people spend money they earned, to buy things they don't want, to impress people that they don't like." ~ Will Rogers.

As we have been looking at the negative personality traits around money and the inherent mistakes they've accrued it's very important to reconcile our money past. This is never about apportioning blame but rather accepting that we did what we did with what we knew or had at the time. Now as we begin to know better, we can do better.

In order to do better we have to let go of the past

mistakes, especially the great big money elephant ones in the room. We've been looking at the pain and the shame around money and some of the antidotes to the behaviour they evoke. It's about simply wiping the slate clean when and where we can AND it's also about taking responsibility and being accountable for the mistakes that have caused harm.

Firstly, we need to forgive ourselves before we seek the comfort of forgiveness from others. The Hawaiian's have a beautiful ritual which is called Ho'oponopono for reconciling the past and offering healing into the present moment to affect the future. This practice works beautifully for self-forgiveness and forgiving others. It's about channelling negative energy into positive outcomes.

The Western popular approach inspired by the Ho'oponopono involves reciting these four things:

1. I'm Sorry — This is not about being wrong or right. It's about humility and recognising that even when we mean the best, or stand firmly in our own integrity, we can still inadvertently hurt others. This is a natural part of being human and acknowledging this is a powerful way to re-examine and reflect on the pillars and values of our own integrity.

2. Please Forgive Me — We free ourselves when we ask for forgiveness. Even if the person we ask doesn't give it right away, we have done all that we can to resolve the situation just by sincerely asking for resolution. The ball is no longer in our court for this particular issue, we have completed our part and remain open for future reconciliation.

3. Thank You — Gratitude is one of the most powerful ways to open the gates of humility and the ability to receive even more life-lessons. Demonstrating gratitude for painful situations or challenges communicates that we are accepting our reality and learning and growing from it. We are emerging stronger and wiser for having weathered the storm.

4. I Love You — Love is the energy that connects us all, it is what animates us to take care of ourselves, our community, and the land. Only from an honest place of love can we accomplish anything of real and lasting value in this world. Yet we often block this energy with unresolved wounds or trauma — especially around money. The essence and intention of Ho'oponopono clears these blockages, returning us to a place of joy, connection, and personal power.

As we look at our financial wounds and feel into the shame and shadow side of our personalities, we may feel deeply uncomfortable. It's a wholesome uncomfortable, some might even say a noble pain, a rite of passage. And it can hurt, and we can feel overwhelmed. This is where again I am urging you to not do this journey alone. Seek professional help if you feel it's appropriate to the pain you are feeling. We often have a challenge about asking for help. Where are you challenged with this and is it time to change?

You can do this challenge with a friend or a group of friends. Trust me ... everyone is in the same leaky boat. Doesn't matter if they are plugging the holes with five cent pieces or hundred dollar bills. We all have money pain.

Journal where you may not have been in true integrity with money. Do you perhaps owe some money? Is money owed to you, but you've been too fearful to address it? Where are you holding any resentments around money issues? Where do you feel betrayed around money or have you yourself betrayed anyone around money?

Again, this is not about making amends ... that's a whole other book. It's simply about unburdening ourselves with the truth of who we are in relation to money. A good safe question to ask is:

'If I were to win the lottery who would I pay back and/or compensate for my past money mistakes?'

~

Practical Money Exercise

Get a copy (copies) of your credit reports or credit ratings - the good, the bad and the ugly. Make sure you get the most comprehensive report without paying a fortune. Some reports if obtained via your bank might be free. You are not penalised for checking your own credit rating/score once per year. This information is important so when you compile your financial autobiography it has a true reflection (for better or worse) of how the wider financial world sees you.

When you get the reports ... you might need to take action to have things removed or amended. Or for most people, it's simply a good record of your spending and lending history. For most people it shows that we are rule abiding and rule responding citizens. For those with a more chequered past it might take some time to process the findings.

Remember this is always about moving forward with Love and Forgiveness. These reports are not a permanent black mark. They are more organic and will start to reflect your better choices as you move more and more into the world with financial acumen.

Sit with the feelings that arise with these credit reports, ratings or scores. Journal what they mean to you. Then write how you feel the world at large, or financial institutions, would judge or see you. Remember we are stirring the muddy waters so that we can eliminate the silt and get clear.

Day Thirteen

Reporting for Action

"God provides the wind, but man must raise the sails." ~ St. Augustine

We are moving towards the halfway mark. It's time to start turning a lot of reflection into action. We should never aim to cease reflection; self-enquiry becomes a great friend and confidant, a wonderful compass as we journey through life. And yet we also need to turn our gaze outwards towards action.

We are going to look at our Credit Reports. Yesterday we obtained them and sat with how we were affected by their content. Today we will look at them with a fine tooth comb and acknowledge what is just and identify what needs addressing. This is akin to the Buddha principle, Chop wood, Carry Water, to simply do what needs doing. No more, no less.

You got a fantastic credit rating and there's nothing to look at here. Everything is in order. That's great and perhaps it subliminally illustrates that you have never taken risks. That you have played it safe. It more than likely indicates that you are the big Banks' dream customer. You pay them what they are owed, fees, interest and charges, and they depend on you. It might indicate you are a money slave to this particular societal and cultural space and time. You might not feel that way at all ... I am just acting as agent provocateur here to make you think outside the box.

As you may have assumed, I am not a fan of credit or loans except for Home Loans — a home is buying physical and emotional security. It also is a tangible legacy to leave in your will and/or asset for retirement. Credit for cars, holidays and jewellery is simply legalised extortion.

Simply write down what the above paragraph conjures up for you. I am not the leading authority on your money, your life or your choices ... but I can be a catalyst for sincere transparent engagement around the subject. I often tell my clients that they have every right to disagree with me, but I encourage them to defend their position, even fight for it. Have the courage of your convictions.

"I don't agree with what you say but I will defend to the death your right to say it."
~ Evelyn Beatrice Hall

If there are discrepancies or inaccuracies in the

report, you will need to address them. This might seem a very daunting affair. It shouldn't be. And symbolically it's more about you standing up for yourself and reporting yourself authentically in the financial world. It matters!

Mr Google, advocacy groups and government websites will help you best navigate the correct departments you need to contact in order to have the inaccuracies rectified. This won't happen overnight but it's worth persevering. It will augment your negotiating skills and it's a project worth fighting for ... your financial reputation. As you reconcile and make peace with your inner financial landscape it makes absolute sense to have the external reflect that too.

What is your credit score? This is the measure of the creditors' belief in your ability to honour your debt in this present moment in time — based on present circumstances and historical statistics. Remember in the age of technology our credit and financial history is available digitally in an instant.

Your payment history is the most significant score influencer. Other things that affect your score are; Bankruptcies, Loan foreclosures, Lawsuits against you, Falsifying Documents. Incidentally, having had no or very little credit goes against you too. Eventually all these financial misdemeanours are eradicated from your file, especially when you turn it around.

The reason that I ask you to do this now is to re-ground you in the reality of money and to empower you not to be afraid of it. Transparency is your friend. Honesty is your friend. Bring it all out of the shadows. What happens to the darkness in an unlit room when we turn the lights on? That's how I want you to see both the physical illusion of your money identity and also the more elusive ego illusion of your money identity.

"Money is a terrible master but an excellent servant."
~ PT Barnum

~

Take a breather. Come back to the breath and the truth of what you are doing. You are making progress, amends, learning a new way, discovering effective strategies, growing, emotionally maturing, healing, and above all creating a brand new way of being in the world with money.

For Australians here is the link to help you find your credit score ... there may be more suited places for you, but this is the best place to start.

moneysmart.gov.au/borrowing-and-credit/borrowing-basics/credit-scores

For other locations, again check on Monsieur Google.

~

Congratulations ... the hardest part is over. You have faced your financial demons. And you survived. And that's what I want you to truly understand and absorb — money troubles are just that, troubles with solutions just around the corner.

In Australia there is fantastic free support for financial troubles. What we are slowly realising is that the problem with money is built into our emotional wiring. No one takes their life because they are in debt ... they take their life because they are afraid, ashamed, hopeless and have immense feelings of feeling unworthiness. Most money troubles are emotional trauma-ghosts running amok throughout our daily lives. Our obsession with wealth and labels and more-more-more is not a financial problem but a human dysfunctional epidemic; a gross perversion of values and worth.

So what are you here for? To recalibrate your values and you're worth. And it's my experience that you will be more valued and valuable when you have true self-worth.

You're doing great ... You got this !

And my final word is avoid credit. Save for things you want ... you'll appreciate them more.

Instant gratification is food for disconnected narcissists.

Mindfully KNEEL before any purchase ... seeing yourself entering a sacred contract and ask these questions:

Know the consequences of this purchase ... what will it really cost me; money, stress, regret etc.? Necessity? Do I need this right now or can I wait? Emotional or Ego purchase? Know that after the initial 'satisfaction' will come a dissatisfaction. Best to hold off? Essential? Food, electricity, gas, car ... Make these a priority.

Luxury or inflated Brand Names? Think very, very hard about this purchase. And think about it as you're walking away from it!

~

Now is a great time to stand up. Shake your body, Make some sounds through your throat from the pit of your belly. Make some noise to celebrate your achievements and make some noise to exorcise any of those money-demons lurking in the shadows.

Don't get too enticed by the story of how you became the person you are today ... spend significantly more time on taking action to forge the person you want to be.

Today I am free of financial troubles ... today I am exploring financial solutions ... today I have never been richer.

Day Fourteen

Give me some credit ... I know what I am talking about here!

"Companies capitalize off people's unwillingness to patiently wait... Top companies understand this demand and respond, "No problem, I will give it to you now, but you will have to pay." — *The Credit Repair Book: The Credit Repair Company's Secret Weapon.*
~ J Cornelius

STOP USING CREDIT.

Earn. Save. Pay.

The only credit you should be leaning on is clean legal contractual family loans for your home and/or bank loans for your home. A home is an emotional investment. It's worth the interest. Although in an ideal world I'd abolish this too; this making extortionate amounts of money from people's need to feel safe, warm and sheltered.

All other credit is pseudo fraud.

The New Ford Focus $24,000 drive away (cash price). The New (will soon be old) Ford Focus) $33,000 Loan Price over 5 years.

Stop putting pride before a fall. It's that simple.

Disclaimer: I am not a financial advisor. I am not legally allowed to offer any financial or fiscal advice. I am simply offering my life experience and the experience of many of my clients who come to me for emotional support on how to deal with crushing debt. Seek real legal advice around your financial hopes, dreams and burdens. And I can really help you understand the self-sabotaging patterns you have around money and image.

'Isn't it obvious Alan what you have to do to help yourself with these crushing debts?' I say to Alan in all earnestness. Alan looks upset, confused and a little vacant as his keyless entry 2019 Maserati GranCabrio lights beckon him into the plush interior. Enough said.

~

If you are in credit card debt or juggling credit card debt, then seek financial help immediately. There are free services in your local community offering debt solutions and strategies. After the Royal Commission Investigation into improper lending, the big Four Banks in Australia have both tightened their lending prerequisites and have also committed to assisting those to whom they have over-loaned.

* The Royal Commission into Misconduct in the Banking, Superannuation and Financial Services Industry, also known as the Banking Royal Commission and the Hayne Royal Commission, was a royal commission established on 14 December 2017 by the Australian government pursuant to the Royal Commissions Act 1902 to inquire into and report on misconduct in the banking, superannuation, and financial services industry.

If you feel that right now you need your credit cards, to pay back Peter to pay back Paul then learn how to manage them better. Go and get help from a financial advisor or financial counsellor. Make a plan and stick to it. Change banks if they are offering interest free credit if you switch to their product. And know that the only reason they offer this is to trap you into paying them the interest and not your former institution. Be the one that slipped through their net and make it work for you.

Credit Card Basics

- What are the fees?
- Are there any large annual fees?
- What are the perks? (Travel insurance and Points but at what cost?)
- What is the grace period before interest is paid? (30 days? 60 days? 72 days?)
- Can you have your credit card interest frozen as you feel your credit limit was raised and raised? Call the bank.
- What is the interest on purchases? Remember this can

be negotiated if you are in financial hardship.
- Pay your card when due and at least 10% more, otherwise you'll never get ahead. Remember it's a trap!

I don't want to get in to financial advice here about how to manage credit card debt … other than drum it in to you that you should get rid of your credit cards and **switch to a Debit Card** — you'll have all the benefits of digital instant online purchasing **BUT** only if you have the funds available.

Another personal tip I can give you is to always wait a minimum of three days before any major purchase. Another trick is to lock your savings away in a high interest term deposit that is not linked to a credit or debit card.

Right now, you're halfway through the feeling and mental process of understanding how you operate in the world with your money. It can be exciting and daunting. Let it all integrate in your psyche and feeling body. You're taking incremental steps to find balance and your own methods to heal from your negative conditioning around money and accentuate what you already do well. It's a process … engage your positivity and gratitude practice. And every time you want to roll your eyes … make sure you're smiling too.

~

Journal about what you are finding in the other part of the book. Write about your money wounds, your money-type and the archetypes that resonate with you. Again … be kind and gentle with yourself. These are self-explorative exercises to free yourself from the illusions that you hold and perpetuate around money. Small change is going to add up to significant growth. Trust, be patient and above all pat yourself on the back for the work done thus far.

Day Fifteen

Beliefs Around Money Boundaries

*"When we fail to set boundaries and hold people
accountable, we feel used and mistreated. This is
why we sometimes attack who they are, which is far
more hurtful than addressing a behaviour or a
choice."* ~ Brené Brown

Today we will look at your belief systems around
friends, family, romantic partners/spouses and money.

As we all come from very different cultures and
socio-economic backgrounds it's impossible to advise hard
and fast rules around who you will borrow money from
and who you will lend money to. Perhaps the safest

financial option is to follow Polonius' advice in Hamlet, Act 1, scene 3.

'Neither a borrower nor a lender be,
For loan oft loses both itself and friend,
And borrowing dulls the edge of husbandry ...'

And yet this is not without complications, expectations and resentments. The truth is money and personal relationships are always a tricky mix. It takes both or all parties to have a maturity around money. A clear and concrete contract with all possible contingencies (mainly death and illness). I urge you to have the difficult conversations. I implore you to spend a little on legal contracts. The flip side of trust is betrayal ... and even the deepest friendships can fall into this polarity trap. Don't risk your love and friendship without very, very clear written agreements. You cannot practise collaborative relating with unreasonable people ... so be kind and make sure both you and the other party/parties involved are not making unrealistic agreements when they are under intense financial and emotional pressures.

The more you know your money-profile the more you will be able to assert boundaries and water-tight agreements with money. And remember it's always best to give from a full cup. So, it stands to reason that the priority is to fill your cup, ensure there are no leaks and fill from multiple streams.

I am not talking here about charity and right action ... only your private and individual moral and spiritual compass can guide you within these realms. However, set the ground rules so that you have something solid to work with.

Journaling Exercises

- What are some of the beliefs you have around lending and borrowing to friends and family and romantic partners? Really examine the way these beliefs make you feel — where in the body do you feel them
- Financial transactions can really amplify our inner money wounds — feelings, fears, paranoia, ultimatums etc. Write down what your shadow side reveals with your belief systems around money loyalty
- Look at where you might feel entitled here … do you believe that parents should bail you out or take care of you? Do you feel richer friends should pay? Would you rather die than ask for financial help?
- Do you owe anyone money? What was the contract and are you honouring it?
- Does anyone owe you money? Again, what was the contract? Verbal or written?
- What situations can you recall whereby money has ruptured a friendship that was unable to be fully repaired?
- Imagine a conversation with the future you, the one who is now well schooled in their money profile? How might they act differently when making financial decisions around friends, family and loved ones?

This is not about making amends right now. In fact, in my experience scantily thought out plans cause more harm than good. Wait until the end of this challenge before you reach towards resolutions. You need to be measured, accurate and realistic in how you go about reparation.

If you hit a particularly surprising spot or scary place … breathe, relax and maybe take a moment. Check in that you feel resourced and resilient enough to continue the enquiry alone. If not, then wait until you are with a good friend or take it to therapy.

Day Sixteen

The Day Dreamer and the incompatible toxic friend, Señor Saboteur

I wanted to combine these two enquiries ... how we dream and how we sabotage our dreams. Most of us have a creative spark and our loyal saboteur talks us out of it, mostly with negative self-talk and negative self-doubt.

Take this wonderful quote ...

"Dream big and dare to fail!" ~ Norman Vaughan

Now give it to your Saboteur ...

"Dreams are for idiots, all of whom have failed"
~ Señor Saboteur

And so, a thwarted life with poverty-consciousness drives around with the hand-break on.

Now I want you to think back to the beginning of this challenge. When we solidified our commitment, where we activated the fire in our belly for change. When we took the most courageous and daunting step, the very first step. Tune in now to your commitment ... how alive is it? How can you reinvigorate this longing for a better life? We are over the halfway mark ... and it's time to dig deeper. We are setting your Dreamer against your Saboteur. Even Albert Einstein said, *"Imagination is more important than knowledge."* There's a man who knows what he's talking about. A man so brimming with knowledge that he knows its true value.

I'll let you into a little secret ... the dreamer is an innate and Divine quality of the human condition. The dreamer always wins in the end. The Saboteur exists only in the realm of illusion and is sustained by fear and self-doubt. The antidote to the Saboteur is imagination, creativity, dreaming and play.

I'll say it again ... loud and proud.

THE ANTIDOTE TO THE SABOTEUR IS IMAGINATION, CREATIVITY, DREAMING AND PLAY.

Let's do some work ...

The Saboteur has many faces and many disguises. We often get so hoodwinked that we have no idea when the Saboteur is directing our movie. As money is literally and metaphorically the most used currency in our lives and power-dynamics it stands to reason that the saboteur infiltrates this medium to overtly or covertly disrupt our lives. It's the easiest way to attack as we have wrapped money into almost every transaction we have. My prayer is that in bringing greater awareness to our emotional and psychological relationship with money that we free ourselves more for kindness, charity, love and connection.

I really want you to get that ... this book is not about being rich or poor — it's about getting your values in the correct order so that you can be in peace and harmony around money, rendering you more effective as a loving, compassionate and heart-centred human being as you navigate your life. And if this book helps you create enough wealth to have the life of your dreams ... than even better. But putting the goal of money and riches before peace and harmony will only accumulate negative consequences down the track. More and more studies show that too little money is stressful and has a negative impact on happiness and inner-peace. Studies also surprisingly reveal that even more negatively impactful is having a lot of money and no inner-peace and harmony to make profitable choices in all areas based around heart-centred values. The clear message here is get your heart, peace of mind and health in great running order and you're more likely to be happy with and without money. Don't we already know this deep down? So why do we keep buying into the fact that it's money that makes us happy.

Happiness makes us money or easy with or without money !!

Enquiry Work

- What are the primary fears you have about you and money? Bring in all the old clichés and borrowed belief systems that you have made part of your psyche or identity?
- How are these fears, big or small, playing out in your life?
- If you were to win the lottery ... what would you do just for yourself? What would you do for family and friends? What would you do for your community or a particular charity?
- If money were no obstacle what business venture might you start? What are you passionate about?
- What does your monkey-mind say about your passions and dreams? Be honest here.
- Are there any destructive behaviours that you have around money that are self-sabotage?
- What are your childhood dreams around being successful or what it means to be happy?
- Where have you lied about money in order to hide or image manage some self-sabotaging act around money?
- Have you let financial opportunities pass you by and felt regret? Especially when seeing friends and family seize the moment and have great results?
- Are you someone who can see easily the financial saboteur in other people's lives? Is this a way of not addressing your own financial-sabotage blind-spots?

After answering these questions I'd like you to go back over them with a fine tooth comb. Peel back the layers ... try and find a place where you are emotionally impacted. A place where you can feel a strong emotion or at least a sense of one ... joy, shame, fear, happiness. Breathe into these emotions and try and sit with them for a few moments or minutes. Again, self-regulate you may need a friend or therapist when processing like this. You may discover something that needs further investigation and you can take that to therapy. Feelings of intense overwhelm, terror, amplified fear/anxiety or collapse are things you might need support with. There's no reason to unpack all of this immediately ... be both brave and measured with your process. Only you will know when you've reached your safety limit.

Looking at our financial Saboteur shows us more intimately how we are with money. How we sabotage the money in our life is how we sabotage our self in life. If you work on this one aspect you can completely transform every aspect of your life. And it's not easy; owning all the ways we hurt ourselves. The Saboteur lives within us. Unless we identify the dark corners he dwells in, we can't ask him to leave.

And we really want him to leave.

Day Seventeen

The Mythical Abundance Secret

There are so many new-age books, seminars, podcasts, blogs and vlogs about how to create abundance. In my opinion abundance simply *is* ... it does not need to be created. We simply need to remove the emotional and psychological blocks in order to receive this life; in all its myriad manifestations.

The illusion that there is some magical secret for health, wealth and happiness belies the fact that life and the human condition will happen to you regardless no matter how rich you are or how many homes you have on tropical islands.

So many people are busy with questions like, *'Are*

you ready for the life you deserve? What does that even mean? Who decides if you're worthy or not worthy? Who is in charge? Who sets the standard of who deserves what and how much? It's ludicrous.

Do I believe that we are all connected, all equal and have the ability to open into this overflowing and ever-changing Existence? YES I do. And I believe more in taking responsibility for your life, your choices, your negative self-talk and your self-sabotaging patterns. If not you ... who?

I love the following quote ... it's deep and worth reverent contemplation.

"If I am not for myself, who will be for me? But if I am only for myself, who am I? If not now, when?"
~ Rabbi Hillel

Life is a miracle. You are a miracle. The moon pulling the tide is a miracle. Birth is a miracle; your birth is a miracle. How cells regenerate is a miracle. Sunrises and sunsets are miracles. Miracles are everywhere and they are free.

Are you getting it? It's your conditioning that weighs you down. And that's why you are doing this work. This tremendous journey of remembering who you truly are. Not this programmed false version of yourself.

While the Laws of Attraction are useful and I believe a lot of them, it all boils down to this when it comes to money ... **"Money is like water, try to grab it and it flows away, open your hands and it will move towards you."** ~ Buddha

This is a great metaphor to being in flow, without stress and panic, and without greed. Be hungry, be ambitious and be progressive with your desires AND never lose focus that a happy soul without attachment to money and things will have more luck (and a lot of it is luck) and of keeping the money.

I am a firm believer in the power of psychology condition healing which in turn changes our thoughts. That's why we are doing this work. We are clearing our self-harming thoughts and stuck detrimental emotions. That's what we can do now, that's what is available to us right now. It's a well-known fact rather than a mystical secret that when we clear out the old, we make space for the new.

Right now, get creative and visionary at what it is you think you would like and then tag this on the end, 'this or something better.' Give Existence some room to offer what's best for you. Demanding and bargaining for your wants and desires may or may not work. But living in a place of trust and open-hearted availability for what life shows you is a far more harmonious and whole-full life.

Give us rain when we expect sun.
Give us music when we expect trouble.
Give us tears when we expect breakfast.
Give us dreams when we expect a storm.
Give us a stray dog when we expect congratulations.
God play with us, turn us sideways and around.
Amen. ~ Michael Leunig

A lot of people talk about keeping your vibration or your frequency high. I understand that to mean clear of redundant and circular negative thoughts. Sometimes that's easy and other times we may need a little help (like this book). But as the Dalai Lama often says,

"Never give up and remember that sometimes not getting what you want is a wonderful stroke of luck."

I like the simple metaphor of housekeeping. Imagine that Abundance is a wonderful guest that you would love to come and stay. Clean the house, prepare great food, have fresh linen on the beds, light fires, chill the champagne, buy or grow fresh flowers ... just be ready for Abundance to drop in unexpectedly. When your attention is on hope and you have space for the new — invariably it will come. And I am a firm believer of literally clearing your house, garden and garage. De-clutter and respect your space and belongings. Give away what you don't need or the things you might need one day.

Do I think it's useful, healthy and healing to create vision boards of your future life? Yes, if it's to help you get clear on what it is you have to do to create it. If it's to put on your altar and simply wait for your good life to arrive, then probably not.

Take charge, take action, have fun, try and fail, make money, take calculated risks ... do all of these things and give a nod to your vision board each morning as you dash out the door chasing reality and dreams.

There are esoteric miracles that I cannot explain. I am not a naysayer. And I encourage the cultivation to stay in the realms of all possibilities. There are plenty of fun and no doubt inspiring abundance activities to embody the feeling of wealth. This changes brain chemistry and can anchor your belief that the new experiences are possible. Athletes use these techniques too imaging a win. Visualisations have their place, but no athlete crossed the finish line eating potato chips and watching daytime television in between the odd meditative visualisation.

In Hadith Qudsi, Allah said: *"O My servant! If you take one step toward Me, I take ten toward you."*

And that's where I believe the simple truth is take the first step towards Abundance and never give up. Take the next and the next and Abundance will accept your loyal persistence.

If we look at what is happening in the brain when we contemplate more in our life, more riches or say more enjoyable experiences, we can see it in understanding the effects of novelty. The mid brain region, the substantia nigra/ventral segmental area or SN/VTA, responds to novel activity or novel stimuli such as thoughts or fantasy. Animal studies around the brain's reaction to novelty have suggested increased dopamine levels. The brain reacts to novelty by releasing dopamine which makes us want to go exploring in search of a reward.

Gratitude is often sighted as a crucial element of '*Abundance*' and has little to do with manifesting in our life and more to do with our mental health. Many studies over the past decade have found that people who consciously count their blessings tend to be happier and less depressed. The great Scientist and Psychiatrist Dr Stephen Porges says we spontaneously experience the feeling of gratitude when our nervous system feels safe. Conversely if we feel threatened or at risk, (read anxiety around survival and lack of money) our thought processes will have a bias towards negativity or depressing thoughts.

Our nervous system is in constant flux of safety, danger or life threat. With money this is felt as…

1. Safety – Money in the bank, confidence in our ability to pay down debt or manage our money
2. Danger – An unexpected expense, like the car has broken down
3. Life Threat – we lose a job, we are left out of a will, our business goes bankrupt

When the nervous system is in a state of healthy relaxation it can perform its job perfectly. It can keep you calm and peaceful and bounce you into flight or fight when called for. By thinking of yourself as a nervous system you should be able to have more compassion for yourself. Rather than '*changing the mindset*', ignoring or avoiding the feeling, our first goal should be to enter a state of self-compassion and respect, witnessing the physiological state that danger or life threat manifests. Then we take our self to a place that feels safer; a walk, a bath, a place where we can meditate and breathe. When we do this repeatedly our nervous system becomes more resilient and resourced taking us back to a place of safety. Only in a state of safety can we begin to manifest our dreams.

Exercises

Ponder these three quotes. Let them settle in you and then give rise to your own understanding of how you can take care of yourself and the people in your world with regards to money. Write in your journal what arises for you; hopes, dreams, practical insights etc.

"There is a thinking stuff from which all things are made, and which, in its original state, permeates, penetrates, and fills the interspaces of the universe. A thought, in this substance, produces the thing that is imaged by the thought. Man can form things in his thought, and, by impressing his thought upon formless substance, can cause the thing he thinks about to be created." ~ Wallace D. Wattles
The Science of Getting Rich

~

The Blessed One (Buddha): *"Suppose a man were to throw a large boulder into a deep lake of water, and a great crowd of people, gathering & congregating, would pray, praise, & circumambulation with their hands palm-to-palm over the heart [saying,] 'Rise up, O boulder! Come floating up, O boulder! Come float to the shore, O boulder!' What do you think: would that boulder — because of the prayers, praise, & circumambulation of that great crowd of people — rise up, come floating up, or come float to the shore?"*
Asibandhakaputta (A man): *"No, lord."*

~ *Tripitaka* Buddhist Scripture
translated from the Pali by Thanissaro Bhikkhu

~

"Nothing in the world can take the place of persistence. Talent will not; nothing is more common than unsuccessful men with talent. Genius will not; unrewarded genius is almost a proverb. Education will not; the world is full of educated derelicts. Persistence and determination alone are omnipotent. The slogan Press On! has solved and always will solve the problems of the human race."
~ Calvin Coolidge

Day Eighteen

Auto-Biography of Spending

"Don't tell me where your priorities are.
Show me where you spend your money and I'll tell
you what they are." ~ James W. Frick

Let's look at the changes you have made and the changes in your spending habits. You've been tracking your spending and it's time to have a good honest look at how you are travelling.

I'd like to say, 'No judgement' and 'everyone is doing their best with what they have.' And I am saying that as well as honouring my commitment to help you once and for all sort out your financials. So, we are judging. But let's get some clarity around the nomenclature here. Usually a judgement is an observation with a charge or a sting. So, we are going to judge fairly and squarely but we are going to take any self-harming charge out and any negative self-sabotaging stings. Remember, we are going to stay with the facts and leave out the dramatic interpretations.

If you haven't already, group all your spendings. Your smart-phone spending tracking app might already do this. If not create the obvious ones first:

- Charity / Altruism
- Personal grooming
- Household items
- Clothes and shoes
- Groceries (food and drink only)
- Entertainment (cinema, magazines, music purchases)
- Eating out at night
- Car — Repairs and Maintenance
- Car — Petrol
- Car — Registration / Taxes / Insurance
- Utilities (gas, electricity, water etc.)
- Telecommunications (mobile, internet, home phone)
- Pets
- Medical
- Gifts
- Mortgage / Rent
- Insurance
- Holidays
- Personal Growth / Seminars
- Yoga / Gym / Fitness
- Coffees / Snacks / Lunches
- Savings
- Bank Fees

This will give you a map of where the money goes. It also gives you a clearer map of who you are; what you prioritise etc. Total each category for one week and have a good look at it. When I did this, I was shocked at what I was spending on coffee, snacks and lunch. I was emotionally eating and also not planning my day's nutrition. Consequently, I lost money and gained weight.

This exercise is only valuable if you dig deep at where you can make changes. If you think you don't need to make any changes, I'd encourage you to find at least one area that you feel could improve.

Self Enquiry

- How does it feel to see your auto-biography in spending?
- Explore some of the feelings in more depth. Is this who you thought you'd be when growing up?
- Are there any clear areas that you know you need to change?
- Is there a deficit that you need to address? Or a surplus that could be better used to grow your money or invest or be charitable?
- How are you feeling in comparison to when you first examined your spending?
- Take those weekly costs and multiply by 52 to see your yearly spending. Any surprises?

Add On

Continue tracking your spending and always practise the KNEEL approach highlighted on Day Thirteen. But this time I want you to track your emotions when spending. Just a simple note such as: Quiet, impatient, rushed, guilty, joyful, self-congratulatory, angry, numb, hurt, sad, bored, neutral, worried etc.

Most purchases will elicit a neutral or minor emotional response. We are particularly looking for the larger impacts. Making the link between the emotional state or motivation before a purchase will truly serve you in this process and your future relationship with money. Making contact with your emotional self before any decision you make will serve you in positive ways you can only begin to imagine.

Day Nineteen

Rolling in the Deep

"Wealth consists not in having great possessions, but in having few wants." ~ Epictetus

Okay ... I get that when Epictetus wrote this back in Greece in circa 55 AD it was excellent philosophy. But he didn't have all the cool stuff that we have in the 21st Century. What were his possessions? An urn or two, a donkey or a goat and a stone hut near the beach? He wasn't busy with iPhones and Pocket WIFI or international air travel and a villa in Florence. But we are ...

The quote still carries some weight and as a good *Billionaire Buddha* you'll find your balance and your very own middle path.

It's time to make a plan. We can be rolling in the deep swirls of money and relaxation or the ashes of debt and stress. We've already made up our minds that we want to free ourselves of the emotional and psychological baggage that keeps us downtrodden. And today we are going to systematically find strategies to tackle debt and make your money work for you.

As I am not a financial advisor, I cannot give you advice about specifics. This is more about inspiring you to research. Make a date with our friend Ms Google and see what help is out there.

Get strategic about reducing, eliminating and re-negotiating debt. It's time to stop procrastinating and just get on with it. There's a time for emotional enquiry and there's a time for pulling up your big girl/boy pants. Today is that day to pull those big girl/boy pants up. Or at least to make a great start and a good to do list.

The Barefoot Investor by Scott Pape gives Australia specific advice about getting on top of your money in a practical way. There's little emotional support or understanding around the psychology of money. But that's why I'm here. It's more a fantastic bootcamp of how to plan and forge a financially sustainable future and retirement. He does give specific strategic 'options' and lets you decide. Always best to read the most up to date publication of his book as he does keep it current.

He'll bring awareness to the fact that there are millions of people in financial crisis and there is a way out.

If you have the emotional stability and mental fortitude to stick to the plan. *The Billionaire Buddha* has been instilling that emotional stability and the mental fortitude within you. You are now ready, or soon will be, to write your plan and stick to it. And sometimes you're gonna need a friend, a confidant or a therapist to walk with you when you're not feeling so resilient. If there's a tired and tested plan … there's always hope.

For example, one strategy of paying off multiple debts is to pay off the smallest debt first while making minimum or slightly more than minimum payments on the others. Then you go to the next one. Clearing debt with high interest is an absolute priority. The mind relaxes and has a sense of achievement and moving forward when one debt is completely cleared. It gives motivation and reward.

Alternatively, pay off the debt with the largest interest first. And always try and negotiate a new interest rate based on financial stress or hardship. You will need to prove this to the financial institute to get an interest fee reduced or frozen. This is perhaps the most intelligent option, but it lacks the emotional satisfaction and creates a feeling of getting nowhere. You can decide on where you think you would have more motivational and feel good success.

Today is about making a new commitment to take all the action you possibly can for self-responsibility around your finances.

As you become more familiar with the language of financial reparation and you find a good book, seminar, friend, accountant, someone or something to guide you through the practical process of financial clarity, you will be well on the road to financial relaxation. How far you go with it is up to you. From a relaxed stress-free space, commit and work hard. Be vigilant, diligent and always do due diligence.

I am always fascinated when people complain about debt and interest rates and how unfair it all is. This is serious cognitive dissonance. If only they had remembered all their complaints whilst making purchases that they can't afford and don't need. And for the record, mea culpa mea culpa !!

Your plan is organic and should always be refreshed and revisited as your financial circumstances change; a pay rise, a redundancy, an inheritance, a lottery win, unforeseen medical bills. This is not meant to scare you but remind you that a broad and big picture is necessary. Let your plan evolve with you.

~

If you're not in any debt you can pat yourself on the back all the way to a financial advisor. Learn how to grow your money in a way that supports your ethics and values. More and more people are choosing ethical and sustainable investments. No point in being financially secure in your retirement on a dying planet. Ask at what cost do you want to be financially secure in retirement?

Get curious and read up on ways to make your money work for you. There isn't just one path but rather many that often criss-cross each other. This is what you're discovering ... who you are around money, values, ethics and heart.

Exercise

Write in your journal a task list around how to research and get the best help in creating a plan.

For example:

- Make an appointment with the local community centre for financial hardship or debt management
- Make an appointment with your accountant
- Take your friend the bookkeeper out for lunch and pick their brains (be transparent with your intentions)
- Talk to a successful friend about what works for them
- Compare the comparison rates on credit cards and transfer rates etc.
- Switch your home loan?
- Downsize?
- Sell the expensive car and buy a good solid reliable cheaper car and throw the difference on a debt or a good investment!

Although I don't want you to get bogged down with the emotionality in this exercise, I will always say that if strong emotions arise, they need to be addressed and cared for.

- When you feel complete with your task list and planning, spend some time imagining what it will feel like when you are out of debt or are living a life that is financially easy. Get that dopamine flowing.

- Think of supportive ways that you can keep yourself

accountable to the task list above. Go at your own pace, and slightly quicker if you can. You can always ease back if it all feels too much.

- Take a long bath or long shower, walk in nature, remind yourself of what a great job you're doing. Be kind to yourself always. Remember the goal is central nervous system relaxation. That's your springboard into the LIFE YOU WANT.

Day Twenty

Essential and Blissful Accounting Awareness

As you iron out and understand the emotional and psychological hindrances in your relationship to money, you'll become more aware of your spending habits. Bringing them from the **Blindful** into the **Mindful.**

A lot of people at this point rebel with ideas and notions that they don't want to be a slave to a budget, or a plan and they want to be spontaneous with their money. And you can be spontaneous with your money; just an allocated portion of it.

If you feel your rebel coming to the fore, then look at him/her/them square in the eyes and let them know that they've been running the show for too long. The rebel here is often seen as the child, the anti-establishment, anti-rules and in short, an instant gratification junkie. You've bought this book so I'm assuming you want my advice? Stop letting your reactive child run the show. Take care of your reactive child but do not let him/her/them direct your life.

Budget can have negative connotations, so we are going to call this part;

Accounting Awareness

Firstly, you must have an **Essential Accounting Awareness** (EAA) spreadsheet or list. This is every cent you need to survive each week — no luxuries and entertainment. In your EAA you must also factor in a small contingency or miscellaneous amount for unexpected costs: car repairs, new vacuum cleaner, vet bill. It's not an amount for all those things but just a token amount to put aside.

Look at your fixed and variable weekly costs and make your EAA based on them. Use your journal and the past exercise to source your information. Remember rent or mortgage payments are fixed and groceries can be variable. Monthly car insurance is fixed, and lunch and coffees are variable.

Be as realistic and as accurate as you can. Look through bank statements etc. Make this as watertight as you can. Factor in birthday gifts for friends and family etc. Think of everything that you spend money on. Add all this up and have a good look at how much it takes to live your life as it stands at the moment. This is your **Essential Accounting Awareness**.

Enquiry

- Any surprises? I am hoping at this stage in the challenge you'll be pretty much on top of your financial biography.
- How are you feeling about your finances and the future right now? More optimistic? Different to when we started? You can't get this wrong. Just be honest whilst checking in to your emotional landscape and where you feel it in your body.

~

Now we are going to look at your **Blissful Accounting Awareness (BAA)**

This is a fine tuning of your EAA with appreciation around what brings you bliss, nourishment and peace of mind. When you are on top of your finances and can allocate a good portion of your money to these elements you will move them into the essential column. Your wellness should be essential. Did you know people spend more money on car maintenance than body wellness? Crazy hey?

But for now ... you are going to see what you can reduce in your variables and use to pay off debt. And when the debt is paid off, you're going to allocate a portion of that money to financial investment or growth, fun and entertainment. To be clear ... you must always have a fun and entertainment fund. But be appropriate to your income. Be smart, make your lunch each day for work and use that money to have more fun. It's simply moving the amounts around to give you a more blissful lifestyle. With awareness around spending you can give yourself little wins every day. This will certainly raise your self-worth and self-esteem.

Have you noticed when children have boundaries, they are more secure in themselves? They can focus more and play wild. Give your financial archetype some boundaries. We are building solid financial awareness in the present, in the day to day emotional and mental relationship with you and money. There will be a time in your research when your Accounting Awareness spills over into the future; into investments and retirement funds. AND you will always be planning for the future in the present moment. Nothing exists but the present moment. We remember the past in the present moment. We anticipate the future in the present moment. So, this course is really about harnessing the present moment.

Some people are far more relaxed when they have an emergency fund. I personally believe it's a good idea for all money personality types. Have a few hundred, a couple of thousand, whatever it is that you can afford and put it in a bank, or with a wealthier friend, somewhere your Instant Gratification persona can't get to it but somewhere that you can access it relatively easily for a major disruption. An emergency fund is usually **3 x your EAA**.

Another conscious way of spending on day to day items is to switch to cash. Withdraw the allocated amount for groceries and stick to it. If at the end of the week it's beans on toast … then let it be beans on toast. Give yourself targets and feel the satisfaction in keeping to them. There's no more sobering experience than literal cashflow.

That's why I am a fan of debit cards. If you don't have the money you can't spend it. In the long run this is the kindest way of managing money until you're truly in surplus mode.

Exercise

* Write out your **EAA** and your new **BAA**. How does that feel?

* Now write out your future **BAA** - one year, two years, five years and ten years from now. Get creative. Really get to see how much you'd like to earn by seeing clearly how much you'd like to spend. It's a great motivator.

* Check in with the fire of your commitment. The aim is to make all of this new information feel like second nature. Remember when you learned to drive? How awkward and clumsy you were? How trying to remember to do a few things at one time felt impossible? And now ... you don't even think about how to drive. Your body and mind drive the car for you while you sing along to your favourite tune. Money can be like this, I assure you. Relax and stay vigilant; isn't that what makes a safe driver?

Day Twenty One

Reach Out or Out of Reach

This is a short simple chapter and yet for a lot of people it's extremely difficult. All the money-types are impacted by this simple reflection. Are you able to reach out for help or do you keep yourself out of reach if help comes your way?

As we've been discovering we have many inherited and learned (often outdated) beliefs and values around money. We didn't have time to try some on and see if they truly fit our personality money-type. Truth is, we didn't know any better. But now we get to choose.

In part of that recalibration we have to accept that we've all probably got a lot of price and image-management happening around money. The amount of shame that can come up around asking for help or even advice can feel overwhelming. We aren't ever really taught about money. Why is that? Why isn't it on every high school curriculum? And yet when we need help around money we are filled with guilt and shame. It certainly feels like a great strategy to keep the rich richer and the poor poorer.

Now is the time to have those difficult conversations with yourself and with those who can help you.

Exercises

- Make a list of all the people who you could pay to help you: financial advisor, bookkeeper, accountant, financial therapist, financial counsellor, psychotherapist, investment property seminars etc.

- Make a list of all your possible contacts or network who would probably help you for free if your humbly asked for their help.

- See what feelings arise in you around paying for help and asking for 'free' help. In this deep enquiry you will face your deepest crystallised conditioning. If you can work on freeing yourself from these crude identity pillars — you will liberate yourself in so many areas of your life.

- Make a list of what's possible for you. Start the difficult conversations with your immediate family, friends and extended network. Even if you just start them in your journal where you feel safe. Then slowly, slowly speak them out.

In my own experience I was amazed who wanted me to truly be happy and get my act together with money. It was like a domino effect of recommendations and generosity. It was incredibly humbling for me and restored my faith in humanity. I had believed for too long that to ask for help was a sign of weakness and an admission of failure. But to ask for help around money issues, well that was tantamount to social suicide. I used to say, *'I'd rather die.'* Now I know I'd rather my very limiting beliefs, conditioning and pride die so that I may live a present and purpose filled life.

Day Twenty Two

Incoming!

Exercise

How much are you paid? Are you happy with your wage? Are you in the right job for your happiness? Are you utilising all your education and skill set? Are you working for great money but are miserable? Where do you prostitute yourself in relation to money? Is it in your work or relationships or both or some other area? When you prostitute yourself around money (which we all do), how do you justify it to yourself? Does low self-esteem or lack of self-worth impact your job choices? What's your dream job? What are you passionate about?

~

~

"You don't have to be great to start, but you have to start to be great." ~ Zig Ziglar

Day Twenty Three

Happiness and Purpose

If you were truly aligned with your life's purpose, then you would be happier. Sure, you'd have to take the rough and the smooth that this human condition affords us. But on the whole, you'd be in a more resilient and resourced place to take the honey and the bitters.

Exercise

- Look into ways to support yourself in realising what your passion and purpose is
- Do you need further study to realise your ideal job?
- What are the qualities and deal-breakers around your ideal job? For example, flexible hours, work from home

sometimes, never working around gambling, not for profits is preferable, with children, not with children, creative etc

- Have you sold out work-wise?
- So many people are resigned in their work roles instead of resigning their work roles. Is this you?
- Do you feel unable to ask for more or simply don't know where to look?
- Maybe you want to work less and be paid more?
- Maybe you want to not work at all? What fear comes up around this question?
- Are you a team player? Or a lone wolf?

Really explore these questions in your journal. Let these questions inspire more questions on the theme. Don't make any dramatic decisions around resignations. All financial income changes are much better handled when planned. Always better to walk out of one job and straight into the next.

We are simply playing around with what really makes you feel you're living YOUR life, that you are in the right lane and your hands are firmly on the steering wheel.

"Working hard for something we don't care about is called stress: Working hard for something we love is called passion." ~ Simon Sinek

Day Twenty Four

Consolidation

"If you choose money over love, you will always be poor." ~ Matshona Dhliwayo

Today is the day of reckoning and consolidation. It's time to look back over the last 3 weeks and take another Selfie. Find a quiet place. If you can somewhere in nature or at least somewhere you can really hear nature. The more senses that are stimulated by this exercise the better. Do this exercise alone. Look up at the sky, day or night. Breathe. We want to try and slow the breath down and get a true sense of yourself both in nature and part of nature. A recognition that you are created with the same fabric as all tangible manifestations in this universe. And that you share so much DNA with most of the tangible and organic manifestations on planet Earth.

This exercise is to ground you in some perspective. As we continue our journey with technological device interfaces and lose more and more live and interactive face time with our fellow human beings, we are being fooled into the ever expanding lie that we are an independent and solitary creature. We are not ... we need social, emotional and physical engagement to feel a sense of belonging, purpose and place in the Universe.

Many people are being treated for depression and anxiety when what they are feeling is isolation, disconnection and possibly an existential crisis. What has this got to do with me and money you might ask? It has everything to do with you and money. You are coming to the end of your dramatic financial makeover, getting ready for this new Selfie, the one you will put up as your profile picture. I want you to really think about that ... 'Who am I?'

Money, in this current societal configuration, is a wonderful way to lubricate connection, altruism, innovation and above all kindness. If you are financially motivated by negative emotions, pride, greed, envy, lack, etc. you will never attain an inner peace. You perhaps will sign enormous financial contracts offering great material wealth, but the small print will always say ...

"Money is no guarantee of true success and heart-felt authentic happiness."

Taking time to reflect what it is you truly want in

this lifetime is the most important contemplation there is. How will you spend your life? Not, how will you spend your money?

Can you have it all … ? YES. YES. YES. Make the money. Make enough money for your wonderful life. Do good business. Do great business. Make money. Make a difference. Make yourself peaceful. Make other people peaceful. Be the TRUE you.

Are you beginning to see that net-worth encompasses so much more than the final figure on your financial summary statement?

This is what you want to write into your new image management portfolio for your new Selfie.

Exercise

- What have you learned about yourself during the challenge? Name at least 5 positives

- What surprised you the most?

- What's the easiest thing you need to change right now?

- What's the most challenging thing you need to change right now? And how can you best support yourself to do this?

- Do you have a better understanding of your particular financial machinations? A deeper insight into you as a conditioned human being who has the potential to re-write that old conditioning?

- How is your commitment, determination and courage to execute change? How do you collapse around this?

- How will you support and nourish yourself towards change?

- How do you feel when 'soaking' in nature?

- What is a good nourishing resource for you? Something easy you can do for yourself when you feel overwhelmed or the negative self-talk comes in: walk, hot bath, run, yoga, tennis, comedy, charity work … etc.

- With your new Selfie firmly in mind … what do you think your friends and loved ones might say about you now, in comparing the old you to the new you?

- Write down what you truly value in your life (not just what is valuable).

- Now on a separate piece of paper write down your new Net Worth. Be as generous to yourself as you can. List your material possessions as well as the unique, colourful, intangible qualities that make up you, kindness, compassion, intelligence, humour etc.

- Weave into this your gratitude and positivity exercises that you are doing each day.

~

~

"Success should be measured by how many people will grieve your loss when you die and not by your current financial gain." ~ Paul C Pritchard

Day Twenty Five

Purse-pose

We have learned in the theory work that our ideas, identities and personality traits are formed in our early childhood and formative years. We've learned that mostly we run on automatic pilot with this 'coding'; it's for the most part unconscious. Most of us never question this operating system unless there's a glitch or a major malfunction. If you're reading this book your life has glitches or malfunctions that you need to address. We have been asking some deep questions around who we think we are, and especially around money. As previously mentioned, money is a great barometer for how we see ourselves and others in the world. We dug deep and set about changing our thoughts and habits around money and transactions. We learned a lot more about who we are, with and without money.

As the new and more awakened *Billionaire Buddha* that you are takes control of your life, by rummaging in your wallet for the wisdom of loose change and the wisdom of large notes, you'll find a new Purse-pose. A graceful way of being with money and purpose.

This chapter is about keeping your purse-pose on track. It's about keeping ourselves accountable. So often we read a book like this when our commitment is strong, and our life demands self-reflection and change. But what happens when the insights pay off and life becomes sweeter again? Usually, we'll hit another wall or a malaise that could feel like a glitch (discontent, bored, lack of direction) or we'll hit another existential crisis (what's the point, futility, not in integrity, not aligned with life's purpose).

The human spirit thrives on safety, expansion and connection. Let's look at these in terms of getting more experienced and wiser with money. We will use these three headers as a way to capture a check list for accountability and also continued progression.

I have this quote firmly set in my heart and mind,

"If you're the smartest person in the room, you're in the wrong room." ~ (Historic Anecdote)

It gives me permission to not be the smartest person in the room. To surround myself with peers and those with greater wisdom than me. I want to keep learning and adding to my knowledge bank. It keeps me humble as well as acknowledging the wins on my own customised wisdom journey. You will customise your own and that makes for a brave new solution focussed world of hope and happiness.

Sense of Safety

* How can I remind myself that having financial security helps me participate in life in a relaxed way whereby I can witness the ebb and flow of life's opportunities and make the correct choices?

* What am I doing for my self-care in order to maintain a healthy body, mind and heart so that I can continue to maintain my financial security?

* What are the areas or blindspots that I fall habitually back into that risk my sense of feeling safe in the world?

* What daily or weekly rituals can I create to keep me on track?

* What do I need to stop doing and who do I need to stop seeing in order to keep my sense of financial safety a priority?

Expansion

* How can I keep growing and learning about money, money management, financial advise and financial security?

- Are there any clubs, support groups, books, podcasts, subscriptions etc. that would keep me anchored to keep exploring my potential?

- Who can I team up with to have constructive, productive and instructive conversations about making money without losing my integrity and heart-values?

Connection

- How can I keep sharing my wisdom to help myself and others?

- What can I do to educate my friends and family so that they too can do better when they know better?

- How can I literally share my money to help create sustainable and regenerative solutions for my immediate community and or my global community?

"A business that makes nothing but money is a poor business." ~ Henry Ford

Day Twenty Six

The Certainties

"Nothing in this world is certain except for death and taxes." ~ Benjamin Franklin

This is probably the only chapter whereby I am really going to offer you some strong advice. How you go about it is of course entirely up to you. I'll be short and 'tweet' (maximum 280 characters).

Taxes

Pay your taxes. Understand your taxes. Be happy to pay your taxes. Put your tax fund in a hard to get at place. Maybe store it in your offset mortgage account. Talk to your accountant. Keep your tax knowledge up to date. Be good to a great accountant. Find a great accountant.

Will

Draft your Will NOW. Get professional advice. Make it watertight. Leave exact instructions for your funeral service. Be fair and let go of old grievances — this is your chance to show posthumous forgiveness. Be generous to those who might need it most. Ask for forgiveness.

"A man who dies without adequate life insurance should have to come back and see the mess he created." ~ Will Rogers

NB: Could also substitute the word a Will instead of Life Insurance.

Insurance

Buy minimum Life Insurance NOW. If still in debt, examine what insurance you have and what is essential. Always insure your own home. Insure your car — comprehensive. Insure you and your family's health. Can't prioritise health insurance? Be Healthy. KNEEL before purchases.

~

In your allocated time for this chapter I want you to start your research about how to get all three things sorted. Don't make any hasty decisions. Shop around and compare the markets. If you are afraid of opening up a can of worms with the ATO (Australian Tax Office), or IRS. Be upfront, see how you hide in the shadows, where is the part of you that does not want to pay to be in community. You might have to start again at the beginning of the book if this is still a problem for you.

Enquiry

Looking at your own mortality and your desire to take responsibility for the way you die and how your legacy is distributed will bring a lot of peace of mind right now. Most people, even if they make very simple Wills, immediately have a sense of relief, especially those who know that they can pay for their own funeral. Basic life insurance is very affordable these days and with monthly payment plans.

Notice what comes up for you around death, taxes and insurance. My advice here is best to practise acceptance. You will have to pay taxes. You will die. And you will have peace of mind right now if Death and Taxes are taken care of.

Until then ...

"Stop acting so small. You are the universe in ecstatic motion." ~ Rumi

Day Twenty Seven

The Four Agreements

I want to recommend this simple yet life changing book, *The Four Agreements* by Miguel Ruiz. I believe that following these four basic tenets for life can strengthen our resolve and our commitment to living a fully aligned life dedicated to **mindful, kindful** purpose.

Here are the four agreements in their essence.

Be Impeccable With Your Word

Speak with integrity. Say only what you mean. Avoid using the word to speak against yourself or to gossip about others. Use the power of your word in the direction of truth and love.

Don't Take Anything Personally

Nothing others do is because of you. What others say and do is a projection of their own reality, their own dream. When you are immune to the opinions and actions of others, you won't be the victim of needless suffering.

Don't Make Assumptions

Find the courage to ask questions and to express what you really want. Communicate with others as clearly as you can to avoid misunderstandings, sadness and drama. With just this one agreement, you can completely transform your life.

Always Do Your Best

Your best is going to change from moment to moment; it will be different when you are healthy as opposed to sick. Under any circumstance, simply do your best, and you will avoid self-judgment, self-abuse and regret.

~

Imagine your life if you applied these four agreements around all your money dealings — things would look very different hey? And in my experience old habits die hard. If you feel you haven't lived up to an agreement, make a note and start again. It's that simple.

Day Twenty Eight

Kindful

It's your last challenge day. Last of the formal *28 Day Challenge* anyhow. Tomorrow you will keep going and continue your learning around life, money and you.

Because of your dedication you will prosper. Congratulations on your commitment, your willingness to dig deep, your longing to make changes in your life and make the world a better place. We have travelled on this *28*

Day Challenge from **Blindful** to **Mindful** and now we expand into **Kindful.**

"Sometimes your joy is the source of your smile, but sometimes your smile can be the source of your joy."
~ Thich Nhat Hanh

Many studies have shown that those who give back and pay it forward are more optimistic and much happier. Human beings are born compassionate and kind. These are default qualities that get buried under fear and hurt. You have been fine financial excavators peeling back the layers to your true self that has been buried deep under the fear and hurt.

You've learned that Positivity and Gratitude build bounce-back resilience. Life is going to keep on happening. You might as well learn to bounce-back with an abundance of fortitude and optimism. So, if giving is a gift to ourselves, let's keep giving and giving to ourselves and giving and giving to ourselves and giving and giving to ourselves ad infinitum. And I know we shouldn't give to receive, but in this case, we can make a loud and proud exception.

There's a misconception around money and giving. Many people are waiting to be generous and kind when they are okay themselves financially. They have goalposts that keeps getting moved as the bills get bigger as the money coming in gets bigger. There's an easy solution. Give 5% of what you earn in supporting anyone who needs it more than you do. I believe this commitment to giving opens the doors to receiving. Try it out. Even in your darkest and most challenging times you will always have something to give, without exception, we always have something to give. If you are in debt or truly struggling, you still have time, prayer and good wishes. And when you can find that 5% or more for charity. No excuses. Practise the art of kindness and watch your worth rise joyously.

"The world breaks everyone, and afterward, some are strong at the broken places." ~ Ernest Hemingway

The world is full of wonderful human beings doing amazing things, big and small, in family and community and on the world stage. I would bet my life on it that ALL of them are strong in the broken places. Be an unsung hero. Be a celebrated philanthropist. Be a closet altruist. It doesn't matter how or how much. You'll discover your own particular way of giving back that fits your own financial Selfie. Something dear to your heart. Some cause that brings you joy. Some research funding that you believe in; medicine, science, the Arts, local community centre etc.

I don't want to end this challenge on a sad note. But I do want to end it on a realistic note. We all need help. We all can give help. We all can do better when we know better.

"Remember there's no such thing as a small act of kindness. Every act creates a ripple with no logical end." ~ Scott Adams

On Going Work

B

The *Billionaire Buddha* — The personal development course that unlocks the wisdom in your wallet. A profound journey into our psychological relationship with money that keeps us stressed, in debt, makes us overspend, links our self-worth with our net-worth and can generally drive us crazy! Check for a course near you, access online courses, connect with the community and more. **TheBillionaireBuddha.com**

Jane Monica-Jones — Jane is available for one-on-one Financial and General Therapy sessions. You can book an appointment via Skype, Messenger or WhatsApp or in her rooms in Sydney, Australia. Just mention **BlindfulMindfulKindful** in your correspondence and you will receive 20% discount from your first session. Or drop her a line for press, media or keynote speaking events. **JaneMonicaJones.com**

SHINE — Have you ever experienced that divine feeling of happy excitement, that open expansive feeling in your heart that life is PURE JOY and that you are PERFECT JUST AS YOURSELF? Where for a moment your head is quiet, you feel playful and effervescent for who you are? If not or only very occasionally then SHINE IS FOR YOU! SHINE a powerfully amazing course. SHINE SUMMIT — Is a soulful mix of Spirituality, Health and Mindfulness. Peppered with practical guidance for work, sex, money body and play. Bringing to together teachers from around the world whose work inspire us to SHINE.
ShineOptimum.com

 Search Jane Monica-Jones for free Guided Meditations and the series *The Dollar Dialogue*

~

Path Retreats — An organisation I have been working with for many years and one of the most profound personal development processes on the planet. It is also coincidentally the place where this book had its genesis. Whilst dealing with a period of severe financial distress and supporting others in being able to face some of their own distress, the idea for *The Billionaire Buddha* came to me in a dream. That there is more to our relationship with money, than just wanting more and as such, set my life on a course of deep exploration of which I could have never imagined the gifts that it has given me and ultimately my clients. My immense gratitude to the *Path of Love* is always with me.

Their signature course the Path of Love 7-day retreat is one of the most intensive and life-changing meditation and

personal development processes in the world today and has gained an extraordinary reputation amongst people who really want to come to know the truth about themselves. It is a profound inner work.
PathRetreats.com

Somatic Experiencing SE by Dr Peter Levine — The Somatic Experiencing® method is a body-oriented approach to the healing of trauma and other stress disorders. It is the life's work of Dr Peter A. Levine, resulting from his multidisciplinary study of stress physiology, psychology, ethology, biology, neuroscience, indigenous healing practices, and medical biophysics, together with over 45 years of successful clinical application. The SE approach releases traumatic shock, which is key to transforming PTSD and the wounds of emotional and early developmental attachment trauma.
TraumaHealing.org

Diamond Approach by A.H. Almaas — The Diamond Approach is a dynamic, evolving teaching that leads to openness, freedom, and realization of the many dimensions of our human potential, especially the amazing secrets of our nature. There are no beliefs to accept or ideology to embrace, you simply need a sincere desire to know what is true about yourself.
DiamondApproach.org

Polyvagal Theory by Stephen Porges PhD — In 1994 Dr Porges proposed the Polyvagal Theory, a theory that links the evolution of the mammalian autonomic nervous system to social behaviour and emphasizes the importance of physiological state in the expression of behavioural problems and psychiatric disorders. He is a Distinguished

University Scientist at Indiana University where he is the founding director of the Traumatic Stress Research Consortium. He is Professor of Psychiatry at the University of North Carolina, and Professor Emeritus at both the University of Illinois at Chicago and the University of Maryland. He served as president of the Society for Psychophysiological Research and the Federation of Associations in Behavioural & Brain Sciences and is a former recipient of a National Institute of Mental Health Research Scientist Development Award. **StephenPorges.com**

Bessel van der Kolk MD — Has spent his career studying how children and adults adapt to traumatic experiences and has translated emerging findings from neuroscience and attachment research to develop and study a range of potentially effective treatments for traumatic. **BesselVanDerKolk.net**

Caroline Myss — Caroline Myss is a five-time New York Times bestselling author and internationally renowned speaker in the fields of human consciousness, spirituality and mysticism, health, energy medicine, and the science of medical intuition. **Myss.com**

Vipassana — The technique of Vipassana Meditation is taught at ten-day residential courses during which participants learn the basics of the method, and practice sufficiently to experience its beneficial results. There are no charges for the courses - not even to cover the cost of food and accommodation. All expenses are met by donations from people who, having completed a course and experienced the benefits of Vipassana, wish to give others the opportunity to also benefit. **Dhamma.org**

~

Stay in Touch

 facebook.com/JaneMonicaJonesPage

 twitter.com/JaneMonicaJones

 instagram.com/JaneMonicaJones

₿

I would love for you to use these tags in your money journey!
#billionairebuddha
#moneywound #moneywounds
#moneymasks

About the Author

Jane specialises in Money, Relationships, Grief,
Addictions, Depression, Anxiety and Trauma.
She has degrees in Financial Counselling, Holistic
Counselling and Psychotherapy, is a trained Anapana Sati
Meditation teacher and a certified Train the Trainer.

Jane is the creator and founder of the completely unique
and profound *The Billionaire Buddha* personal development
course that shifts our relationship with money to
transform our life.

Her other bodies of work include *SHINE, Enter the Flow -
Intuition Training, Money Wound Counsellor/Coach Training,
Anxiety Free* and *Depression Free.*

JaneMonicaJones.com

Jane Monica-Jones

BONUS

Simply quote the code: **BlindfulMindfulKindful**
To receive **20% OFF** any of my other books, content,
courses or sessions ... **FOREVER!**

For **Financial Therapy** sessions just mention the code in
your email and you'll get the discount for that too.

NOTES

NOTES

NOTES

NOTES

NOTES

NOTES

NOTES